A LIGHT TO ALL NATIONS

Fr. Brian Thomas Becket Mullady, O.P., S.T.D.

A LIGHT TO ALL NATIONS

On the Nature and Mission of the Church

EWTN Publishing, Inc.
Irondale, Alabama

EWTN Publishing, Inc.
5817 Old Leeds Road, Irondale, AL 35210

Distributed by Sophia Institute Press, Box 5284, Manchester, NH 03108.

paperback ISBN 978-1-68278-405-1

ebook ISBN 978-1-68278-406-8

Library of Congress Control Number: 2024934423

First Printing

To Mark Andreas and Frank Dulcich
without whom this work
could not have been written.

Table of Contents

INTRODUCTION

Ecclesia, quid dicis de te ipsa? (Church, what do you have to say about yourself?)[1] Before John Paul II became Pope, he wrote a book, *The Sources of Renewal*, on the proper understanding of Vatican II. According to him, this question is the key to understanding the Council. Chapter 4 is entitled, "The Consciousness of the Church as the Main Foundation of Conciliar Initiation."[2] As a bishop who was present at the Council, imbued with the trust and teaching of Vatican II, he pointed out that the whole conciliar project can only be understood as a great self-examination on the part of the Church. "It is impossible to treat the Church merely as an 'object'; it had to be a 'subject' also. This was certainly the intention behind the Council's first question: *'Ecclesia, quid dicis de te ipsa?'*"[3]

There have been many books written on the teachings of the Second Vatican Council and on the subject of the Church as treated in one of the two principal dogmatic constitutions, *De Ecclesia* (On the Church) also known by the first two words, *Lumen Gentium* (*The Light of the Nations*).[4] Though this Council was indeed an event that the Holy Spirit directed in the life of the Church, the implementation of the documents was a problem even while the Council was going on. Immediately before the Extraordinary Synod that produced the *Catechism of the Catholic Church* and celebrated the twentieth anniversary of the closing of the Council in 1966, Cardinal Ratzinger gave a now-famous interview in which he expressed the frustration of the whole Church about this Council. For the first time, an authority openly stated that what was being taught and done in the Church in daily practice did not fulfill the intention of John XXIII in calling the Council.

> What is certain is that the Council did not take the turn that John XXIII had expected [...] It must also be admitted that, in respect to the whole Church, the prayer of Pope John that the Council signify a new leap forward for the Church, to renewed life and unity, has not—at least as yet—been granted.[5]

It seems that no one is really satisfied with what has been happening in the Church since Vatican II. For some, it went too far. For others, it has not gone far enough. What is certain, though, is that very few people really have a clue as to what the actual teaching in the documents is. This has allowed a strange interpretation to develop, especially in universities and seminaries, that evokes a mythical "spirit of the Council" to justify departure from the real text of the Council. Cardinal Ratzinger defines it thus:

> Already during its sessions and then increasingly in the subsequent period, was opposed a self-styled "spirit of the Council," which in reality is a true "anti-spirit" of the Council. According to this pernicious anti-spirit [*Konzils-Ungeist* in German], everything that is "new"... is always and in every case better than what has been or what is.[6]

The famous conciliar theologian Henri de Lubac, S.J., noted a similar difficulty in the reading of the documents. He called it the "para-Council."

> Just as the Second Vatican Council received from a number of theologians instructions about various points of the task it should assume, under pain of "disappointing the world," so too the "post-conciliar" Church was immediately and from all sides assailed with summons to get in step, not with what the Council had actually said, but with what it should have said. [...] This is the phenomenon which we should like to designate as the "para-Council."[7]

This "para-Council" has basically hijacked what the Fathers at Vatican II specifically taught on many subjects. "What the para-Council and its main activists wanted and demanded was a *mutation*: a difference not of degree but of nature."[8] This is true of all sorts of problems in the post-conciliar period. It is especially true of the whole idea of the Church.

For this reason, it does not seem out of place to examine the document on the Church again from a fresh perspective. The perspective I have chosen has a twofold source. First, I use the interpretive device of the Aristotelian-Thomistic division between Being and Act. Though it is perhaps true that the Council Fathers rejected a too abstract and Scholastic approach to doctrine, this does not mean that one cannot apply the terms and categories of *philosophia perennis* to the teaching of the Council. Pope John Paul II has indicated anew in *Faith and Reason* that the approach of classical philosophy is necessary for an understanding of theology. I think this hermeneutic will give greater clarity about the organic teaching in *Lumen Gentium.*

Secondly, I will use a rich mine, rarely tapped, to explain what idea the Fathers of Vatican II themselves held of the Church. This is the *Synopsis Historica* (henceforth *SH*) of the *relatio* (report) that the doctrinal commission provided for all the parts of the document.[9] The *Synopsis Historica* is of great value because it provides specific notes of the commission on why they used all the various expressions which were used, including the sources for their use of these expressions.

This will be my primary source, together with the *relatio* of Bishop Gasser, which was used by the Fathers in Vatican I as the authentic interpretation of the teaching on the infallibility of the Pope. Vatican II found much its teaching on collegiality in this document.[10]

It is my hope that these two new contributions to the discussion, together with the clarifications made by the Holy See in various documents since Vatican II, will provide a synthetic, clear presentation of the constant teaching of the Church on the nature of the Church. One of the prime difficulties in post-Vatican II books on the Church has been a lack of logical method and order. But the very document of the Council supplies a wonderful order and method for understanding the Church.

Meditation on the Church is the final chapter in a long development of doctrine which began in the earliest councils with clarification of the apostolic teaching concerning Christ. In fact, according to a very recent address given by Pope John Paul II to the Conference for the Implementation of the Second Vatican Council, the purpose of Paul VI was precisely to treat of the Church of Christ in homogeneous development with all the previous doctrine which had been taught, including Vatican I. "'The time has come when the truth about the Church of Christ must be explored, set in order and expressed,' (*Insegnamenti*, vol. I [1963]), pp. 173-174. With these words the unforgettable Pontiff [Paul VI] identified the Council's principal task."[11]

This means that the self-examination of the Church must include all the definitions, common teachings and philosophical tools the Church has had at her disposal throughout the previous centuries. This is a powerful truth and must be the basis for launching the final implementation of Vatican II to the world of the Third Millennium. What a wonderful way to OPEN TO DOORS TO CHRIST, YESTERDAY, TODAY AND FOREVER, LIGHT OF THE NATIONS!

CHAPTER ONE
The Structure of the Document
The being and act of the Church

All studies depend on the subject matter, which in turn gives rise to the methodology of the study. This is true of the study of the Church that the Fathers of Vatican II conducted in *Lumen Gentium*. The doctrinal committee clearly stated the order when a question arose whether to treat religious life in one chapter with the universal call to holiness, or in a chapter on its own. The commission's solution to this problem summarizes the order for treating this matter, and the reasons for the order are very interesting.

In this chapter, I will first treat those reasons, examine the order of the document and finally show how this order perfectly fits the Scholastic distinction of the primary and secondary act, or being and act, as explained by Aristotle and St. Thomas Aquinas. In a later chapter, devoted exclusively to the consecrated life, I will discuss in a more formal way how this treatment contributed to the Council's doctrinal proclamation on the Church. [12]

When the Council members asked whether one chapter could treat both the universal call to holiness *and* religious life, those favoring the single chapter argued that an opinion had arisen in the Church stating that holiness was reserved to those who professed religious life. They therefore wanted religious life to be seen as an eschatological sign within the Church herself and as a charismatic sign that always exists in the Church and proceeds from the essence of the society of the Church. There were three reasons, then, for a single chapter.

The first reason was theological: The Fathers wanted to show that the distinction between the clergy and the laity is an essential structure in the Church. [13] But religious are a structure within the Church and not of the Church itself. The second reason was pastoral: The Fathers argued that many Catholics felt religious held a monopoly [14] on perfection and sanctity. A single chapter, they said, would better teach the truth that religious life must be seen in the perspective of the more universal holiness of the Church in general. The third reason was ecumenical: Many of the leaders of the Protestant Reformation wanted to destroy an invisible wall that they perceived the Catholic Church as having erected between religious and the laity, as though the two were called to two different kinds of holiness. One chapter would help to answer this common objection to religious life.

Another group argued that treating religious life in a separate chapter from the universal call to holiness would emphasize that religious life has a special place[15] in the constitution of the Church. They also said that a separate chapter would clarify the importance and specific aspects of religious in the Church.

They further maintained that the logical order demanded that one treat in the first place the purpose and holiness of the People of God, and *then* the diverse functions and states of life in the Church in which this holiness is realized. This separate chapter would demonstrate that religious are not accidental to the Church.[16]

The commission and the Council in general decided on two chapters. They reasoned that the order of exposition found in the first part of the document, which distinguished the People of God in general from the various individual vocations, should be observed in a second part of the document by distinguishing the faithful's common participation in holiness from the specific, individual charism of religious life. Just as the distinction between the People of God and their varied participation in the hierarchy was essential to the divine institution of the authority of the Church (and founded on a difference between the character of baptism and the character of Holy Orders), so the distinction between religious and others arises from the universal and particular vocations in living the life of holiness which is the purpose of the Church.

Lumen Gentium's treatment of holiness distinguished between the nature of the Church in itself and the characteristics of the Church as the People of God within the society and their relationship to other religions. Finally this general treatment ends with the specific differences between the hierarchy and the laity.

Corresponding to these distinctions are the different ways people realize the purpose of the Church as a society. This is holiness. First, the universal call to holiness is discussed, then the religious life, and finally the completion of the Church in its final consummation, heaven. The document ends with a discussion of the Church's chief exemplar, Mary.

The doctrinal commission specifically developed the following order:

Chapter 1: "The Mystery of the Church," which considers the "divine order and intimate nature"[17] of the Church.

Chapter 2: "The People of God." This chapter treats of the pilgrimage of a new People—a new society of God on earth—in the common exercise of the universal priesthood and also explains the sense of the faithful in believing (*sensus fidei*)[18] and those charisms that are characteristic of the Church as a whole. It also treats of the universal or Catholic unity of the Church and relates this union of society to other Christians and other religions.

Chapter 3: "The Hierarchial Constitution of the Church and Specifically the Episcopate." This treatment emphasizes the place of the bishops as the successors of the Apostles. Vatican I wanted to define the role of bishops, but the political situation in Europe cut the Council short without its ever being formally closed. (In fact, John XXIII formally closed Vatican I before Vatican II opened.) Here the bishops are seen to derive their authority from their ordination, but they exercise this authority always as one "Body or Order with one Head, the Supreme Pontiff."[19] Together, the Pope and the bishops exercise the office of Christ as priest, prophet and king, always aided by priests and deacons.

Chapter 4: "The Laity." This chapter discusses the laity, the other great pivot in the hierarchy of the Church. The Fathers taught in this chapter that the laity were not lesser in Christian dignity, but shared Christian dignity with the hierarchy. They cooperate with the hierarchy in the saving mission of the Church according to Christ as priest, prophet and king. They do this by Christian obedience and faithful harmony.[20]

Chapter 5: "The Universal Call to Holiness in the Church." This chapter now turns to the end (*finem*)[21] or purpose of the existence of the Church as a society. This is the universal call to holiness and perfection in all the various forms in which Church members pursue it, including the evangelical counsels. By the recommendation of

Our Lord, the evangelical counsels of poverty, chastity and obedience are to be pursued by everyone in the Church according to one's vocation.

Chapter 6: "Religious." This chapter specifically treats of those who pursue these three counsels by some formal vow or promise in total consecration. This pursuit is always under the authority of the Church and involves some sort of formal state of life whereby a person wants to follow Christ more perfectly. This is called religious life. This chapter discusses the place of religious life in the Church as a present witness to charity and as an eschatological sign of the future life. The Fathers hoped to increase esteem for this state as well as point out the difficulties in living it.[22]

Chapter 7: "The Eschatological Nature of the Pilgrim Church and Its Union with the Heavenly Church." This chapter concerns the final consummation of holiness, which is in the glory of heaven. This is where the Church is perfect and complete, when God is all in all. The union between the Church in final fulfillment and the Church here on earth is also addressed.

Chapter 8: "The Godbearer, the Blessed Virgin Mary in the Mystery of Christ and the Church." This chapter rounds off the whole discussion of the nature of the Church with a special consideration of Mary, the Mother of Christ, who is also the Mother of the Church. Mary is the motherly and virginal model for the Church (*maternalis et virginalis typus*). This final chapter was intended to recapitulate the complete exposition of the mystery of the Church as a final flourish (*coronidis instar*)[23] finding its example in the mission of the Blessed Virgin in the Church.

The obvious structure of *Lumen Gentium* truly corresponds to proper methodology in treating first of the nature of the Church (being) as a society with its properties and then of the purpose or action for which the being of the Church exists (act). This structure applies a traditional metaphysical division of the matter of a thing into being and action. As a thing is, so does it act. *Operari sequitur esse.*

According to this division, there would be two completions in being present in each natural thing. The first is that it exists with all of the fullness of nature. The second is that its existence realizes a further perfection in action. The potentials or potencies, present in the very existence of a thing, can only be realized by further actions.

For example, when someone is born, he or she has intelligence, and if all of his or her faculties are intact, he or she has the perfection possessing the power of intelligence. But this perfection of nature (or first perfection) exists so that individuals may actually know (second perfection). They cannot do this unless they experience something and apply a process of reasoning to it. The same would be true of the leg or the eye. Someone might be born with these intact and be able to walk or see, but until someone actually walks or sees, these powers are not really perfect. St. Thomas Aquinas expresses this distinction between first and second perfection (being and action) often. For example:

> The perfection of a thing is twofold, the first perfec-
> tion and the second perfection. The first perfection
> is that according to which a thing is substantially
> perfect, and this perfection is the form of the whole;
> which form results from the whole having its parts
> complete. But the second perfection is the end, which
> is either an operation, [...] or something attained by
> an operation. [...] But the first perfection is the cause
> of the second, because the form is the principle of
> operation.[24]

This division between being and operation, or first and second perfection, applies not only to natural beings, but also to moral beings like societies. The being is the given form of the society, the act is the purpose for which the society exists. The purpose (or end) of the moral union distinguishes one society from another and provides the means to attain a social end (e.g. the authority unique to that society). This is because society is formed by a moral union of wills pursuing a common goal.

The society of the Church is a supernatural society because it has a supernatural purpose. The purpose of the Church is to participate in the society of the Trinity here on earth through faith, hope and charity, and in the next life through the beatific vision in which the Church will be perfected. As this is a goal beyond the capability of the human will left to itself, such perfection can only be pursued by the aid of grace given from above. Thus, the Church as a social union can only be caused by grace. The study of the Church, then, must have its origin in divine revelation, and the standard for examination of the Church cannot be mere human reason.

The order of study in *Lumen Gentium* demands first a treatment of the Church's supernatural character. This is done in chapter 1. The medium of demonstration is the term "mystery" or "*sacramentum*," which distinguishes the Church from every other human society. In chapter 2, the being of the Church is more specifically treated by establishing the characteristics of this society on earth and then comparing and contrasting it with other societies. The medium of demonstration in this chapter is "People of God," a term inherited from Old Testament Israel to mark the Church as a special society.

In chapter 3 the character of the Being of the Church is further developed by examining the nature and order of the hierarchy. Here the medium of demonstration is "communion" among the members of the college of bishops, and their relationship to the Pope and the laity. Chapter 4 examines the same relationship from the point of view of the laity. This relationship includes an exposition of the rights of the laity *vis-à-vis* the hierarchy.

The Act of the Church follows on the basis of its Being. If the structure of the Church should be perfectly present, this is only the perfection of form (or being) and then is ordered to action. The eye may be perfectly formed, but such an organ only attains full perfection in the act of seeing perfectly. The structure of the Church exists solely for the actual living of the life of grace by all the members of the Church, both the hierarchy and the laity.

Chapter 5 deals with charity, the act of grace that all the hierarchy and the sacraments exist to elicit from the members of the Church as a whole. This charity is the source of our merit in heaven.

Individuals are called in a special way to live the life of charity by sacrificing even the legitimate goods of this world because these goods would compromise the complete freedom to act from God's point of view. This is not only for an individual's own sanctification, but as a stimulus to everyone in the Church to desire the final perfection of heaven. Chapter 6 deals with those who are called to this special way in the consecrated life.

Chapter 7 points out that the action of the Church is not completed in faith, hope and charity. Because man has an intellect, he cannot be content with knowledge of faith, hope and charity; he must experience God directly. St. Teresa is reputed to have said, "I am dying because

I do not die." The society of the Church can be completed only in the next life by the Vision of God. Until then, the Church is in pilgrimage on earth. Note that this pilgrimage does not touch the Being of the Church as expressed in her hierarchical structure, but is treated in the section on the Act of the Church. Sometimes people presented the pilgrim character of the Church as referring to her hierarchical structure as though that depended on the spirit of the age. The Church, for example, might now be better expressed as a constitutional monarchy as this better responds to the needs of modern man.

Finally, the Act of the Church is most graphically seen in her members. The first among these is Our Lady. Chapter 8 treats of the life and faith of the Blessed Virgin as the summit of the Act of the Church.

The order of treatment then of the divine society of the Church is:

THE BEING OF THE CHURCH

CHAPTER 1: THE CHURCH AS MYSTERY

CHAPTER 2: THE CHURCH AS PEOPLE OF GOD

CHAPTER 3: THE CHURCH AS HIERARCHY

CHAPTER 4: THE CHURCH AS THE LAITY

THE ACT OF THE CHURCH

CHAPTER 5: THE CHURCH AS HOLY IN GENERAL

CHAPTER 6: THE RELIGIOUS LIFE AS A STIMULUS TO THE HOLINESS OF THE CHURCH

CHAPTER 7: THE HOLINESS OF THE CHURCH AND THE VISION OF GOD

CHAPTER 8: THE BLESSED VIRGIN AS THE MODEL OF HOLINESS IN THE CHURCH

PART ONE
THE BEING OF THE CHURCH

CHAPTER TWO
The Supernatural Being of the Church

The Church is a mystery. The primary task of the Council was to clarify this mystery by developing the doctrine of Vatican I on the nature of the Church. "In those pages we brought to completion the doctrine expressed by the First Vatican Council and *we sealed it for a renewed study of the Church's mystery*."[25] The word "mystery" is used in the title of the first chapter of *Lumen Gentium*, together with the word "sacrament," which is its Latin equivalent. Some Council Fathers objected to these terms because they feared they would confuse the faithful, leading them to think the Church was a sacrament in the strict sense of the seven sacraments. Some use the word "mystery" merely to express something which cannot be explained.

The Church is not a sacrament in the strict sense of the word, as the seven sacraments are, causing grace *ex opera operato*—from the performing of an action. Here the term emphasizes that the Church is a society in which the communion of persons found among the Three Divine Persons of the Trinity is made present to us here so that we can participate in it.[26] "The Church, then, both contains and communicates the invisible grace she signifies. It is in this analogical sense, that the Church is called a 'sacrament.'"[27]

The Church is not a mystery simply because it cannot be fully known. The term "mystery" emphasizes that the Church is not an earthly society as we ordinarily define such an assembly.

The purpose of the Church is participation in God's light. Christ has brought us the ability to do this, so he is the "Light of the Nations" (*Lumen Gentium*). Here "nations" means all peoples of the earth in every time and place.

> The Church is at one and the same time: a "society structured with hierarchical organs and the mystical body of Christ; the visible society and the spiritual community; the earthly Church and the Church endowed with heavenly riches." These dimensions to-

gether constitute "one complex reality which comes together from a human and a divine element."[28]

The key concept to understanding the mystery of the Church is that of communion (*koinonia*), which is "at the heart of the Church's self-understanding."[29] This communion is a true participation in the society of the Trinity, which is the result of the presence of sanctifying grace in the soul. Grace is something in the soul. Catholic tradition echoes St. Thomas Aquinas, affirming that grace is an entitative habit of being that elevates the soul to partake in the very nature of the Trinity. "[...] Man is aided by the gratuitous will of God because some habitual gift is infused in the soul by God.... Therefore, the gift of grace is a kind of quality."[30] The Catholic tradition has seen in this habit of being an expression of the text of the Second Letter of Peter: "[H]e has granted to us his great and very precious promises, that through these you may escape from the corruption that is in the world because of passion and become partakers of the divine nature" (2 Peter 1:4). The Greek word for "partakers" is *koinonoi*, which is obviously related to *koinonia*.

Christ introduces the light of grace into the soul of the Christian, thus establishing a relationship in being with the Trinity. The kind of being is that of a quality, rather than a substantial change in man. Grace is a plus added to human nature to allow us to partake in the divine. Man is truly sanctified, but his nature is not substantially changed into God's nature. Yet his soul is qualitatively elevated so that he can know as God knows and love as God loves. He is so elevated so that he can view all, the inner life of the Trinity and the ordinary life in the world, *sub specie aeternitatis* (under the aspect of eternity).

Communion of the person with God is therefore a communion with the Trinity; this forms the ontological basis for the communion on earth among the society of believers. The Church has a human structure because on earth it is made up of people (*koinonoi*) who experience communion (*koinonia*) with God by grace. This society has a purpose that transcends earth, though it is on earth. As such, the members on earth of the community of the Church are formed and participate in the life and mission of the Persons of the Trinity.

In the first paragraph of chapter 1, the Conciliar Fathers expressed these two aspects of the Church as mystery. "[...] the Church, in

Christ, is in the nature of sacrament—a sign and instrument, that is of communion with God and of unity among men."[31] In the next three paragraphs, the Fathers relate the being of the Church to the various missions of the persons of the Trinity,

The missions outside the Trinity reflect the processions in God. For St. Thomas a "mission" is a new manner of God existing in the world of creatures in time, reflecting the character of the relations within the persons in God in eternity. This new manner necessarily relates to our sanctification. The divine mission "includes the eternal procession, with the addition of a temporal effect."[32] The Father is not sent in mission because he is the First Principle and origin of the Son and the Holy Spirit. As the Father sends, the nature and action of the Son and the Holy Spirit in time reveal something hidden about the Father and his relation with the other two persons and their relations with each other. The Son, together with the Father, sends the Holy Spirit. Thus the priority of origin is the source for the authority of the Son respecting the Holy Spirit.

> ...Whoever sends has an authority over the one sent. One must, then, say that the Son has authority in regard to the Holy Spirit: not, of course, that of being master or being great, but in accord with origin only.[33]

The Son and the Holy Spirit have both invisible and visible missions. These missions reveal the inner nature of the Trinity to us because they reflect the inner relations of the Persons in God.

> Thus, the Son is said to be sent into the world inasmuch as he began to be in the world in a new way through the visible flesh he assumed ... He is also said to be sent to someone spiritually and invisibly inasmuch as he begins to dwell in him through the gift of wisdom.[34]

> Of course, the Holy Spirit visibly appeared; "as a dove" (Matt. 3:16) above Christ at his baptism, or "in tongues of fire" (Acts 2:3) above the Apostles. And, granted that he did not become a dove or a fire as the Son became man, he nevertheless did appear

> in certain signs of his own visible appearance of this
> kind: thus, he also in a new kind of fashion—namely,
> visibly—was in the world.[35]

The purpose of all the missions of the Persons is the final invisible mission of the Holy Spirit, which is the sanctification of man. Since the Son sends the Holy Spirit (because together with the Father, he is the principle of the Holy Spirit together with the Father—or if one prefers the orthodox terminology, the Father sends the Holy Spirit through the Son), the invisible mission of the Son in time is absolutely necessary to the sanctification of souls.

In each of these paragraphs in chapter 1, the notion of mission is explained insofar as these missions are connected to the nature of the Church. In paragraph 2, the Fathers explain the Father's act of sending: creation, the call to holiness and the sending of Christ as a remedy for the Original Sin. The call to holiness implemented in Christ is the basis for the existence of the Church, which encompasses all holy people from the beginning of the world.

> Already present in figure at the beginning of the
> world, this Church was prepared in a marvelous fash-
> ion in the history of the people of Israel and the Old
> Covenant. Established in the last age of the world,
> and made manifest in the outpouring of the Spirit, it
> will be brought to glorious completion at the end of
> time. At that moment, as the Fathers put it, all the just
> from the time of Adam, "from Abel, the just one, to
> the last of the elect" will be gathered together with
> the Father in the universal Church.[36]

In paragraph 3, the Fathers explain the mission and place of the Son in this foundation. They teach that the Son is continually present in his visible mission in the Church, which is an extension of his body. The Church was founded ontologically when the blood and water flowed from the side of Christ on the cross. Christ founds the Church through the visible organization of the sacraments, for the water symbolizes baptism, and the blood, the Eucharist. "The Blood and Water that flowed from the pierced side of the crucified Jesus are types of Baptism and the Eucharist, the sacraments of new life."[37] The Fathers end by affirming the universal primacy of Christ, for the sacraments receive their power because they are extensions of the flesh of Christ throughout time and space, and they have the same power as his flesh, though as separated instruments.

> As in the Person of Christ the humanity causes our salvation by grace, the divine power being the principal agent, so likewise in the sacraments of the New Law, which are derived from Christ, grace is instrumentally caused by the sacraments and principally by the power of the Holy Spirit working in the sacraments.[38]

In paragraph 4 this section concludes with several points about the mission of the Holy Spirit, which is to sanctify the Church. The Holy Spirit prays in the hearts of the faithful and gives witness about the Son. The Holy Spirit unifies the Church by communion (*koinonia*) and ministry (*diakonia*). Since there is a unity of communion and ministry, the hierarchical offices are among the gifts the Holy Spirit gives to the Church.

This introductory section concludes with the bold statement that establishes the being of the Church as a supernatural society. "Hence the universal Church is seen to be 'a people brought into unity from the unity of the Father, the Son and the Holy Spirit.'"[39] Though it has an earthly aspect, it is a mystery. This means that the Church must have both a vertical and a horizontal dimension, and one cannot be sacrificed for the sake of the other.

In fact, the communion of the society of the Church is based on communion with the Trinity as its source and end.

> If the concept of communion, which is not a univocal one, is to serve as a key to ecclesiology, it has to be understood within the teaching of the Bible and the patristic tradition, in which communion always involves a double dimension: the vertical (communion with God) and the horizontal (communion among men).[40]

Those who receive sanctifying grace as members of the Church enter into communion with God. This communion is the source of the communion of the Church as a society.

As the Church is not merely an earthly society, but a sacrament, a mystery which has a visible form pointing to something beyond the physical sensible world, the next task is to apply the idea of a supernatural society to several images of the Church. The first is the image most used in the Gospels: the Kingdom of God. The Fathers used this image first because in their view it most clearly demonstrated the truth that the Church was both a visible and a spiritual society, with both an eschatological aspect fulfilled after this world and an historical aspect in this world of time. This image is fundamental to the whole concept of the Church expressed by Vatican II.[41]

> The Church is essentially both human and divine,
> visible but endowed with invisible realities, zealous
> in action and dedicated to contemplation, present
> in the world but as a pilgrim, so constituted that in
> her the human is directed toward and subordinated
> to the divine, the visible to the invisible, action to
> contemplation, and this present world to that city yet
> to come, the object of our quest.[42]

The Kingdom of God is brought into this world by Our Lord in both his words and his works. His words point to the actions necessary to prepare for the Kingdom; his works show us the power of the kingdom to give us eternal life. This life is rehearsed in all the various miracles Our Lord performed, with respect to physical nature, and completed in his elevation of fallen nature to grace on the Cross and in the Resurrection. This Cross and Resurrection were accomplished in his body and the attitude of loving obedience in his human soul, and thus the establishment of the Kingdom and Church shines forth especially in his Person.[43] Though he is one Person, he is at the same time divine and human.

Christ completes the establishment of the Kingdom in his person by personally sending the Holy Spirit to dwell in the unique society of the Church.[44] The Holy Spirit guides the Church here on earth and prepares her for her final consummation in heaven. This necessary participation of both the Son and the Spirit in the completion of this society perfectly expresses the doctrine of the missions.

Vatican II wanted to emphasize a renewal of interest in Scripture in the Church, and Scripture uses various images to emphasize different aspects of this primary image of the Kingdom of God. These images culminate in the great image of the Mystical Body of Christ.

The first images are taken from the Old Testament. The Church as an engraced society is founded on the initiative of God. God goes out to look for sinful man and cares and heals him, guiding him back to his home as a shepherd does his sheep.[45] Images taken from agriculture (especially that of the vine) show that the Church is constantly subject to divine care, and so continuously grows.[46] Images drawn from building teach the progressive and firm structure of the Church.[47] God continuously preserves this society against the ravages of time. Finally, the image of the bride[48] expresses the spousal dimension of Christ and the Church: the place where one experiences intimacy of communion with God and expresses this communion in faithful obedience to the will of God. The Fathers return here to the theme of the completion of that spousal union in the glory of heaven.

These themes are all consummated naturally in the great image of the Mystical Body of Christ. Some interpreters of Vatican II had the idea that the only image used by the Council was that of the People of God. This image seemed to provide a whole new aspect of the Church, which might free her from a hierarchical nature (or at least a hierarchical interpretation). However, the theme of the Mystical Body is altogether contrary to the attempt to reduce the Church to a human society with spiritual overtones. But the Council cannot be used to justify such an interpretation. The theme of the Mystical Body is treated in paragraph 7, before the theme of the People of God, and both images are necessary to understand the Church.

> [...] We also have in mind the link between the Mystical Body of Christ and the People of God. The Church is at the same time both one and the other. In *Lumen Gentium* the picture of the Church as the People of God is perhaps the more prominent. But in the Council's teaching as a whole we find sufficient reason to affirm that the People of God is also the mystical Body of Christ, and to throw light on this theological identity. It is the reality of the redemption that helps us to do this. The consciousness of the redemption is logically prior to the consciousness of the People of God. [...] If we proceeded too

> rapidly from the theme of the redemption to that of
> the People of God, the latter would not appear to us
> in the fullness of its significance. In this case one
> might speak here of a unilateral "sociologization"
> of the concept [...] the vertical dimension being
> overshadowed by the horizontal.[49]

The Catholic Church is the Mystical Body of Christ. This image first states that this society has its origin in the redemptive offering of Christ and the Cross. It also expresses the ordered and hierarchical elements of both the interior and the exterior elements which make up the Church. The Church is a supernatural society, with different members, all united by the same sacraments and gifts of the Holy Spirit, given and sustained by the power of Christ.[50]

The faithful are introduced into the Mystical Body by the sacrament of Baptism, and sustained in the life of Christ by the Holy Eucharist. In both sacraments they are conformed to Christ the Head who died and is now risen in glory. These sacraments make our souls holy, conforming them to the life of Christ, and so sanctify even our bodies.[51]

Since each member is unique, the Mystical Body has an order among the individuals who make it up. All the members are gifted supernaturally with the gift of grace. Each expresses this gift differently by his own unique gifts and charisms. The charisms characteristic of each vocation are distributed by the Holy Spirit, but under the authority of the hierarchy, which has its own role to play, because Christ is the head in his visible nature and acts through the Spirit in the members.

The headship of Christ is seen first in creation and then in the Church. The members are conformed to him in the Passion and Resurrection and grow by allowing him more and more to influence their lives. This influence demands preparation and disposition in free will to receive the growing love of the Holy Spirit in our daily lives. God gives himself in freedom in Christ and the Spirit; man freely accepts this gift by preparation and cooperation and the two become one flesh, as it were. Bride and Body become one in the Mystical Body through this ever-growing union of love. In this, Vatican II echoes St. Paul in his letter to the Ephesians, Chapter 5.

Give way to one another in obedience to Christ.
Wives should regard their husbands as they regard
the Lord, since as Christ is the head of the Church
and saves the whole body, so the husband is the
head of his wife. [...] That is the way Christ treats
the Church, because it is his body—and we are its
living parts.[52]

Lumen Gentium ends the initial reflection on the supernatural
being of the Church by identifying this heavenly community with the
community begun on earth. The earthly community, which shares in
the communion of the Holy Trinity, is known to us through the senses
and can be experienced in everyday life while on earth.

The Church, whose intimate and hidden nature has
been described, in which she is perpetually united
with Christ and his work, is concretely found on this
earth in the Catholic Church. This Church which
we experience in our senses reveals the mystery,
but not without shadow, until she is led into the full
light, as also Christ the Lord attained glory through
emptying himself.[53]

The mystery of the Church is present and experienced in a concrete society. The visible structure and the invisible reality are not
two things, but one complex reality,[54] at the same time a medium and
fruit of salvation. The Mystical Body mirrors the reality of the Person
of Christ, who is also not divided into two things, but is one complex
reality, divine and human, in the unity of his Person.

This does not mean that the Church has a monopoly on the visible elements (such as the belief in one God, the natural law, a love
for Scripture) that can be means to experience the mystery of God.
Though the Church, as the Kingdom of God/Body of Christ/Com-
munion of saints/Bride of Christ is present uniquely in the Catholic
Church, other religions share common elements with her.

Moreover, the Church on earth is made up of both saints and
sinners and so is peculiarly strong with grace, yet filled with weakness. Thus, she is "at the same time in a condition of poverty and
persecution, of sin and purification."[55] In this she is also conformed
to her Master, though he was without sin. Where does the Church

look for hope in this condition? She must look to Christ, to his power and love.

The Church that Jesus established while on earth is thus identified with the supernatural society that is communion in the life of the Trinity. This Church is further identified with the Church as she exists today in the Catholic Church. The Council declares: "The Church constituted and organized as a society in the present world, subsists in the Catholic Church, which is governed by the successor of Peter and by the bishops in communion with him."[56]

This line sums up the chapter, and introduces two important themes dear to the Fathers in Vatican II but much misunderstood in the aftermath of the Council. The first of these themes is the relation of the Catholic Church, in which the Church "subsists," to other religions. The second is the nature of communion. Both are vital for the rest of the treatment of the being of the Church.

Some have maintained that by saying the Church "subsists in" the Catholic Church, instead of saying that it "is" the Catholic Church, Vatican II was at least soft on the unique and necessary role of the Catholic Church in salvation. These critics suggest that the Catholic Church enjoys a role of *"primus inter pares"* (first among equals) common to political ideas about democracy. In this view, Christ could be looked upon as one, but not the unique, mediator of salvation. There might be many others, such as Buddha, Gandhi or Mohammed. Or, if one did believe that Christ occupied a unique place, one might think that one Christian community that claimed to be a Church was as good as another, provided one believed in Christ. This error was described in the 19th century as indifferentism, the notion that religion should be indifferent to dogmatic expressions. What should matter instead was the feeling of dependency on God and philanthropy to neighbor. As long as a given religion stimulated this feeling of dependence and philanthropy, what one believed in that religion was not really important.

The Congregation for the Doctrine of the Faith summarizes this[57] erroneous opinion well in the recent declaration *Dominus Jesus.*

> The Church's constant missionary proclamation
> is endangered today by relativistic theories which
> seek to justify religious pluralism, not only *de facto*

but also *de iure* (or in principle). As a consequence, it is held that certain truths have been superseded; for example, the definitive and complete character of the revelation of Jesus Christ, the nature of Christian faith as compared with that of belief in other religions, the inspired nature of the books of Sacred Scripture, the personal unity between the Eternal Word and Jesus of Nazareth, the unity of the economy of the Incarnate Word and the Holy Spirit, the unicity and salvific universality of the mystery of Jesus Christ, the universal salvific mediation of the Church, the inseparability—while recognizing the distinction—of the kingdom of God, the kingdom of Christ and the Church, and the subsistence of the one Church of Christ in the Catholic Church.[58]

In fact, *Lumen Gentium* used the word "subsists," not because the Council wanted to deny the unique and necessary place of Christ and the Church in salvation, but because it wished both to affirm this traditional belief and extend the hand of ecumenical friendship to other religions.

The Council wanted to proclaim two truths: One was the unique and necessary importance of Christ and the Church, identified with the earthly community governed by the Pope, and the other was that there are elements outside the Church that are means of salvation. "Some words are changed: in place of 'is,' 'subsists in' is used, as this expression better accords with the affirmation about ecclesial elements which are present elsewhere."[59] The earthly Church with the Pope at her head is identical on earth with the heavenly Church, but as a pilgrim in this world. Other religions have teachings that they share with the Catholic Church, and these can be a valid means to salvation both inside and outside the Church. So, the use of the term "subsists in" was not meant to deny the unique character of the Catholic Church, but rather to emphasize that other religions share some elements with the Church that are true and good.

With the expression *subsistit in* [subsists in], the Second Vatican Council sought to harmonize two doctrinal statements: on the one hand, that the Church of Christ, despite the divisions which exist among Christians, continues to exist fully only in the Catholic Church, and on the other hand, that "outside her structure, many elements can be found of sanctification and truth," that is, in those Churches and ecclesial communities which are not yet in full communion with the Catholic Church.[60]

Some think this position is contradictory; others would like to use this section of *Lumen Gentium* to justify indifferentism. The seeming contradiction can be resolved if one remembers that *Lumen Gentium* is distinguishing between partial truth mixed with error and full truth. Catholics are sometimes accused of thinking that no one else can be saved. This is not true. To the extent that one is not responsible for knowing that the fullness of the truth exists in the Church and uses the positive means available in his religion, he can certainly be saved. This doctrine is based on two distinctions: invincible ignorance that one morally cannot help, and the emphasis on those means that the Church herself uses. These means are always found together with others in the Church that lead to the fullness of truth. "But with respect to these, it needs to be stated that 'they derive their efficacy from the very fullness of grace and truth entrusted to the Catholic Church.'"[61]

How and when members of other religions receive grace from these means is a question Christian theology cannot answer. The possibility is there because these religions are all implicitly connected to Christ in some of their teachings. Two points must be stressed, however. This grace must be received in this life because no one can merit anything after death and the most basic implicit faith demands that one at least believe "that God exists and that he rewards those who seek him."[62] In other words, an atheist or someone who does not believe in some sort of afterlife cannot have even implicit faith in Christ, no matter what good he could do for the world.

Nor is this doctrine emphasized by Vatican II a new doctrine. Fr. Bede Jarrett exhibited a common acceptance of it in spiritual talks he gave long before Vatican II.

> An older generation startled us by telling us that all other religions contained in fragments what the Catholic Church held in a complete form, but found on examination that this was one more reason for

acknowledging the truth of revelation. If the Christian Faith were really divine, then surely man must feel deeply the needs that it comes to supply, and, in consequence, will feebly and brokenly grope his way toward them. Because I can find every single doctrine of the Church taught by some religion or other, and because I can find them gathered together nowhere else than in her, then surely I am convinced that she has obtained, by the swift light of God, what they painfully and falteringly have partly discovered. Surely, then, this should give me a greater realization of the importance of my soul.[63]

In 1955, before Vatican II met, Cardinal Journet gave a similar, but more theologicial statement of these truths.

It is important to note here that when we say that the Church is in formation outside the Church, we are looking at things in a way which, from the ecclesiological standpoint, is accidental and secondary. We mean that those who broke with the Church [and *a fortiori* those who are not yet members] took with them certain good things which by their very nature belong to her. In themselves, in virtue of their own internal exigencies, these scattered fragments demand to be reintegrated in the Church, and we know that the universal saving virtue of the God of mercy works mysteriously and incessantly for their reintegration. But clearly this reintegrating movement works in precisely the opposite direction to the original movement by which the dissident Churches cut themselves off from the true Church. Outside the Church, the Church is in formation, but this comes about accidentally, by violence done to the course things have taken. Outside the Church, the Church of itself is in decomposition. Any fragments of life broken off from her are no sooner detached from their native whole and subjected to the influence of the principle of dissidence, than they begin to disintegrate and decay.[64]

The Council concludes this foundational chapter with an examination of the fulfillment of the mystery of the Church. The Church progresses in this world towards fulfillment in heaven in contradiction and opposition like her Head. This consummation will occur only in the heavenly Church, a theme that will be examined at great length in chapter 7 of the document. The actual triumph of the Church cannot occur on earth. As the Church is a mystery, a sacrament of invisible realities, a society based on the society of the Trinity, this consummation can occur only in the beatific vision of God where all is "wholly communion and feast."[65]

CHAPTER THREE
The People of God

Perhaps no term in Vatican II has led to more misunderstanding than the term that is the title for this chapter: The People of God. This term has been taken by many to mean an exclusive emphasis on the horizontal nature of the Church and, even more, to suggest that all are equal with respect to authority in the manner of a liberal democracy. It was common around the time of the Council to hear those who discussed it say that the Mystical Body of Christ had now been changed to the People of God. They would draw a descending triangle with the Pope at the top and descend through cardinals, bishops, priests, religious and end with the faithful. Then they would cross this out and merely put God—People of God. In some places, the People of God came to be distinguished from the hierarchy, which was identified with the enemy or a thoroughly nasty tyranny, against which the People of God was engaged in an heroic struggle.

Furthermore, this term was often used to deny the unique character of the ministerial priesthood. With the cry, "We are Church," many believed this term justified a completely new collegial Church. The term "college" (which is actually formally treated in the next chapter) was used to justify treating the Church as a parliament and the Pope as a constitutional monarch, with a primacy of honor, but not one of jurisdiction. Finally, this collegiality was taken to apply to all institutions in the Church, not just the episcopacy, so that even superiors in religious orders had no true authority, but had to act in a collegial way. All was now a democracy.

As I have shown in the last chapter, the term "People of God" was in no sense intended by the Council Fathers to deny the hierarchical nature of the Church expressed in the term "Mystical Body." Rather, the term "People of God" is used to examine the general nature of the Church, to distinguish the Church from all other religions. The term therefore reflects the participation of the Father in the earthly Church, and was used as the basis to compare and contrast the Catholic Church with all other religions, pagan and Christian. This comparison does not address hierarchical distinction, but reflects all the members of the

Church, clerical or lay. The term cannot be used to play off hierarchy and laity against one another in some kind of strange Marxist "class warfare," nor to justify looking on the Church as a parliamentary democracy, because it includes all the members, each in his or her own function. "'The People of God' is not here understood about the flock of the faithful as though it were distinguished against the hierarchy, but embraces all, whether Pastors or the faithful, who pertain to the Church."[66]

Vatican II in no sense meant to detract from the truth that there is a certain precedence of the hierarchy with respect to the laity. But the Council did teach that this precedence was a means in relation to an end, which was the holiness of each member of the Church, hierarchy and laity.

> If it is true that the Hierarchy in a certain aspect go before the laity, in whom they beget faith and supernatural life, it nevertheless remains that the Pastors and the faithful pertain to one people. The People itself and its salvation are in the judgement of God in the order of an end, while the Hierarchy is ordered as a means to that end. The People should be considered especially in its totality, so that then both the office of Pastors who present the means of salvation to the faithful and the vocation and obligation of the faithful, who, conscious of their personal responsibility should collaborate with the Pastors for the diffusion and complete holiness of the whole Church, is more clearly shown.[67]

In sum, then, the treatment of the People of God does not address the question of the distinctions *within* the Church, but rather speaks to the issue of the members of the Church as a whole, in their relationship to the other religions, including non-Catholic Christian religions. The biblical term "People of God" expresses primarily the unity and universality of the Church, and then describes how this Church is connected to the rest of the human race.

In paragraph 9 of chapter 3, *Lumen Gentium* formally takes up the question of the formation of this people or "commonwealth of God" as a society in history, starting from the premise that God does not just will to save individuals. His salvation is promised to man in the

Protoevangelium, Genesis 3:15. Speaking to the serpent, God says, "I will put enmity between you and the woman, between your seed and her seed; he shall bruise your head, and you shall bruise his heel." This promise is made in the context of the punishments enumerated for the Original Sin. Since the Original Sin entailed a moral act, the two greatest punishments were ignorance, in the intellect, of God's inner life; and malice, in the will towards others, expressed especially in manipulation and abuse of others.

The sign of the presence of the Original Sin is that man is proud both of his intellect (or knowledge) and his will and freedom (or power). After the sin, man tried to resolve the difficulties of his soul with both his own knowledge and his own power, and came up against a wall in each. So, to remedy for human ignorance, God gave the Old Law in the time of Moses on Mount Sinai, a law not given just to Moses, but to the entire Israelite people that they might be a "commonwealth of God." "As the precepts of human law order man to human community, so the precepts of divine law order man to a kind of community or commonwealth of man under God."[68] This is the formal institution of the Church, though all the just are included in the society of the Church.

This Old Law taught what was right and so cured the punishment of ignorance, but in itself it could not cure the will because it did not give grace. The people of the Old Law knew what was right, but the whole history of Israel is replete with examples of those who understood the commandments but broke the most important one, monotheism, by syncretism. And even if they affirmed this commandment by religious practice, the prophets frequently decry the fact that their social justice to neighbor did not correspond to their professed love for God. God allowed this condition to continue to convince the Jews, and through them the whole human race, of their need for a Redeemer. This Redeemer would complete God's revelation and also truly write the law on the hearts of God's people. He further would establish this community's final perfection on earth.

Christ completes this commonwealth in a spiritual sense when he founds the Church through his own body and blood, by remedying the malice in the will by his perfect and loving obedience. The Community of the New Law of Christ is directly established by him through his various acts on earth and finally completed only in heaven. The community of the Church is thus a "visible sacrament of unity."[69] This unity transcends the divisions of human communities and cultures throughout the whole world because it is a direct union with the Persons of the Trinity and preparation for a goal which is not realized on earth or in an earthly way: the vision of God in heaven. "Woman, believe me, the hour is coming when you will worship the Father neither on this mountain nor in Jerusalem. [...] But the hour is coming, and is now here, when true worshippers will worship the Father in spirit and truth, for the Father seeks such as these to worship him." (Jn. 4: 21, 23)

In both Israel and Catholicism, his holy society is characterized by two expressions of the priesthood. In Israel, people became members of the commonwealth or People of God in two ways: the laity became consecrated by circumcision; the priests, by ordination. In the Church of the New Testament, the laity are consecrated by Baptism; the priests, by ordination. In paragraph 10 *Lumen Gentium* takes up this unique social expression. Both the People of God in the Old Testament, and the People of God in the New, are characterized by two distinct consecrations: the general consecration of membership, and the ministerial consecration special to the ordained priesthood.

Vatican II wanted to examine the general priesthood of the laity in order to emphasize that there is a consecration and holiness unique to every member of the Church, and that the heights of the spiritual life are not reserved only to the clergy. There is a fitting emphasis on the general consecration of the whole People of God in Baptism, in which all are called to imitate Christ as priest, prophet and king. This consecration comes through the character or indelible mark given to the faithful in Baptism; it is strengthened in Confirmation. The fullness of the consecration is conferred by the sacrament of Holy Orders, which allows the recipient to consecrate the Eucharist. Still, the laity are priests because they help to make the family holy, especially in the sacrament of Matrimony, of which they are the ministers. They are prophets because they are called upon to teach the truth, especially in the family. They are also kings because they must rule their lives by grace. The order of the document speaks first of the priestly role (paragraph 10), then of the kingly role (paragraph 11) and, finally of the prophetic role (paragraph 12).

All the faithful are truly priests through Baptism, but their priesthood differs from the ministerial priesthood, "essentially and not only in degree."[70] Yet, "the one is ordered to the other."[71] The ministerial priesthood, though it involves the power to define doctrine on the episcopal level, to govern the earthly Church and to consecrate the Eucharist, is only a means to the end of the holiness and consecration of all the faithful. The clergy are the means ordered to the end, which is the faithful. They are the servants of the faithful. All clericalism reverses this truth. Clericalism looks on the laity as the servants of the clergy.

The faithful have their own part to play in the celebration of the Eucharist by offering themselves and their lives and allowing Christ, through the power of the sacraments, to influence each day. This is what is meant by active participation (*participatio actuosa*) recommended by Vatican II in *Sacrosanctum Concilium*, the document on the liturgy.

The kingly role of every member of the Church consists in ruling his life, in charity, by the constant development and practice of the virtues. Those who offer themselves in the liturgy and receive Christ must allow the moral life of his Sacred Heart to influence both their reception of the sacraments and the daily life of their state. An ancient saying goes: That man is most powerful who can rule himself. Every member of the Church must rule himself in holiness. This kingly role is lived especially in the family when parents guide their children to fullness of life.

> Strengthened by so many and such great means of salvation, all the faithful, whatever their condition or state—though each in his own way—are called by the Lord to that perfection of sanctity by which the Father himself is perfect.[72]

The faithful are also bound to believe and tell the truth; this is their prophetic role. God has given each member of the Church this mission according to his state. Teaching the truth cannot be left to priests and sisters, or to an educational elite. The faithful have always been considered infallible in believing, provided they follow the manner of discovery of the faith established by Christ: Scripture and Tradition, with the Magisterium as their servant. The only faithful who enjoy Magisterium and, thus, teaching authority, are the Pope and bishops. "The People of God, guided by the sacred teaching authority (*magisterium*), and obeying it, receives not the mere word of men, but truly the word of God."[73]

Though the whole People of God is infallible when they all adhere to the same doctrine, this does not mean that bishops must listen to the laity and formulate doctrines according to a kind of consensus or "common ground." Rather, the Magisterium of the bishops determines the common ground in the Catholic Church. The supernatural character of the Church is clearly seen in the supernatural knowledge at the basis of the faith which forms her. Faith, hope and charity, which are given to each member of the Church in Baptism, form the basis of this consecration. This consecration based on grace, which forms certainty of faith about those truths which hold the Church together, is expressed in the universal consensus (*consensus universalis*)[74] of all the faithful in believing a given truth. When the faithful as a whole believe a doctrine, they cannot err in expressing it, but this consensus "as a whole" includes the bishops and the papacy as well as the laity, each in their own measure contributing to this belief.

Many in the post-Vatican II Church have used this truth of the Council to justify a democratic idea of the Church in which the voting majority should determine doctrine. Many also wrongly believed that this democratic idea was an innovation in Vatican II. The documents themselves provide many reasons why these opinions have no foundation.

The Council is clear that universal consensus is not a question of the laity arriving at a decision and the bishops accepting this common ground as the truth. This is because the consensus must include the hierarchy. "One treats here of the whole People of God, including the Hierarchy."[75] The infallibility of the Church as a whole, in believing, is common doctrine taught long before Vatican II.

> The greatest post-Tridentine theologians (M. Cano, St. Robert Bellarmine, Gregory of Valencia, Suarez, Gonet, Billuart), clearly taught the infallibility of the faithful in believing. The manner of proceeding in their exposition and argumentation is often explicitly "from the faithful to the Hierarchy," or from infal-

libility in believing to infallibility in teaching; and in this they did not see any danger to the Hierarchy. There does not even seem to be any danger in asserting that the consensus of the faithful must be considered by the Roman Pontiff.[76]

The *sensus fidelium* is not a kind of democratic common ground that must be respected by the hierarchy in making definitions of faith, a kind of credal truth by plebiscite. Instead, the *sensus fidelium* refers to the fact that the whole of the Church can discern between the true and the false in matters of faith precisely because it is a supernatural community. But there is no judgement on who has the right to define this discernment.

This supernatural judgement is not applied only on the level of belief, but also enters into life through supernatural practice. In practice, the divine character of the Church as a society is expressed not only "through ministries and sacraments,"[77] but also in the ordinary virtues and in all the charisms given by the Holy Spirit to the Church, both ordinary and extraordinary. The Church as a People is enriched by each of these gifts, though the extraordinary ones must not be "rashly desired."[78]

Lumen Gentium clearly teaches that the authority of the Church should not stifle any of these charisms, even the extraordinary ones, but it also teaches that these charisms do not judge themselves. The authority of the Church is charged with the mission of testing and judging these charisms. So, not only does the Council affirm that the Church is not a parliamentary democracy, but it also denies any claim to have a fuller manifestation of the Spirit than the one given to the hierarchy. A prime characteristic of this new kind of divine society is the disavowal of all Gnostic movements. The prophetic character of the People of God and all claims to special inspirations of the Holy Spirit, including private revelations, must be judged by the hierarchy, which has been entrusted with this task.[79]

Another characteristic of the People of God is universality. The Church is not a particular society in a particular part of the world, but one universal society because the call of faith is to the whole human race. The foundation of the universal bond is the charity that is given directly by God and fills the human heart. Though this unity is

of heavenly origin, it takes place in an imperfect way in the hearts of
the faithful on earth. The whole human race is related to this society
in some way.

Since the Church is a universal and supernatural society, there
is no one universal culture that can express all the riches of the
Church; cultural diversity is imperative. Not only would the denial
of cultural diversity seriously impair the spreading of the kingdom,
but such a denial would also suggest that some earthly form could
fully express the Trinity. Exaggerated order in any human society is
destructive because the individual is swallowed up. The same is true
of the Church.

> From the beginning, this one Church has been
> marked by the great diversity which comes from both
> the variety of God's gifts and the diversity of those
> who receive them. Within the unity of the People
> of God, a multiplicity of peoples and cultures is
> gathered together.[80]

Since the unity of the Church is based on the unity of the Persons
of the Trinity, and yet is sacramentally expressed here, it is "at once
both transcendent and immanent."[81] This is why the Church can respect cultural difference and at the same time affirm the necessity of
unity in doctrine, sacraments and life.

Though the Church affirms the necessity and possibility of
cultural diversity, this does not mean there are no common cultural
characteristics that all Catholics share. Nor does it mean that there
are no elements in a culture that need to be purged if that culture is to
express the Gospel. The Church is never so allied with any one culture
that it cannot stand as counterculture in those things that may be at
odds with reason and the natural law. All things truly in accord with
right reason may be of use to the Church in the spread of the Gospel.
Each culture taken up into the communion of the Church must by
this union be "purified, strengthened and elevated."[82]

Nor is this cultural diversity so important that it can undermine
the unity of the Church around the See of Rome. This communion
in the Trinity finds visible union in communion among the local
churches—individual dioceses and parishes, not national churches or
episcopal conferences—with each other and with the Chair of Peter

(a term that emphasizes primacy of jurisdiction to teach doctrine), "which presides over the whole assembly in charity."[83] The ministries and religious orders serve this divine communion and find their *raison d'etre* in strengthening it.

So universal is this communion in God that all men have a necessary relationship to it. Christ has come to save the whole human race, so every person living has some relation to this communion. This is because the Church is the Mystical Body, and all men are related to it. Yet, a Mystical Body is not a natural body, and so this Mystical Body may have people who are only potentially or partially members.

> There is the difference between the natural body of man and the Church's mystical body, that the members of the natural body all fit together, and the members of the mystical body are not all together; —neither as regards their natural being, since the body of the Church is made up of men who have existed since the beginning of the world until its end;—nor as regards their supernatural being, since, of those who exist in any one time, there are some who are without grace, yet will afterwards obtain it, and some who have it already. We must therefore consider the mystical body not only as they are in act, but also as they are in potentiality. [...] Christ is the head of all men, but diversely. For, first and foremost, He is the head of such as are united to Him in glory; secondly, of those who are actually united to him by charity; thirdly, of those who are actually united to him by faith; fourthly, of those who are united to him merely in potentiality [...][84]

The general examination of the People of God in relation to other societies, cultures and religions demands a clear description of basic membership in the Church after the coming of Christ, and a general treatment of how other religions, both Christian and non-Christian, relate to this society. Catholics who are "incorporated" into the Church show certain characteristics necessary for this incorporation; others are not "incorporated" but "conjoined."[85] In *Lumen Gentium* this necessary distinction is addressed in three paragraphs. The first refers to the incorporation of the faithful (paragraph 14); the second to non-

Catholic Christians (paragraph 15); and the third to non-Christians (paragraph 16).

Since the Church is the visible community on earth, which participates in the communion of the Trinity in heaven, "the Church, a pilgrim now on earth, is necessary for salvation."[86] Since Christ proclaimed the necessity of faith and Baptism, this necessity includes the Church. Those who knew that the Church was the Mystical Body of Christ and the visible sign of communion with the Trinity and "refused to enter it or remain in it [...] could not be saved."[87] This does not mean that others cannot be saved. Those can be saved who are in invincible ignorance that the Church is the means of salvation.

Who, then, is fully a member of the Church? Following the distinction made by St. Thomas about how Christ is the Head of his Mystical Body, one must say that only those who believe in everything taught by the Church, who are in the state of grace (possessing the Spirit of Christ),[88] and are in communion with the visible structure presided over by the Pope and bishops, are fully members of the Church. This faith and communion includes three elements: profession of faith, the sacraments, and ecclesiastical government.[89]

There was some discussion in the doctrinal commission in Vatican II as to what word to use to express these requirements for the faithful. Originally the terms, "really (*reapse*) and simply (*simpliciter*)" had been used. The commission felt that these were "obscure (*obscura*) and even not right (*non recta*)."[90] Commission members decided to use "fully" (*plene*) instead, because they did not want to exclude baptized children who had not yet reached the age of reason, or even ignorant Christians who were not intelligent enough to know and fulfill every condition.[91]

The term "in reality" (*reapse*) for those who enjoy full communion goes back the *Mystici Corporis*, the famous encyclical of Pius XII on the Church.[92] Pius XII makes a distinction in this encyclical between those who are really members of the Church and those who are only members *in voto* (by desire). Vatican II so distinguishes here, and adds that those who are catechumens are members of the Church in desire.[93] Obviously, the catechumens have the baptism of desire because their "explicit will"[94] is already to enter the Church and receive baptism. There is no judgement made here about limbo and certainly no reflection of the "anonymous Christians" or good pagans. This is left to another paragraph. The delineation of the faithful is clear and explicit. The only reason one could be saved without acknowledging all the truths the Council teaches is invincible ignorance because anything else would involve something morally impossible.

The same requirements are listed in the Catechism and the Code of Canon Law.

> But the pilgrim Church is also assured by visible bonds of communion:—profession of one faith received from the apostles;—common celebration of divine worship, especially the sacraments;—apostolic succession through the sacrament of Holy Orders maintaining the fraternal concord of God's family.[95]

> Those baptized are in full communion with the Catholic Church here on earth who are joined with Christ in his visible body, through the bonds of profession of faith, the sacraments and ecclesiastical governance.[96]

From this is it clear that the Council teaches in accord with all Catholic tradition that only those who accept all of the dogmas of the faith are fully members of the faithful and thus form the People of God. This was proclaimed in the previous chapter, when the Church was identified with the Catholic Church (paragraph 8).

Other Christians are related to the faithful in different ways. These Christians either do not believe in, or are not in communion with, the "Chair of St. Peter."[97] In both cases, though, these Christians have many objectively positive connections with the People of God. Nonetheless, these connections are characterized either by a lack of faith or by a lack of communion.

Those who lack faith do so in varying degrees, and though they are our "separated brethren," they do not truly constitute a Church in the proper sense of the term. These include the various Protestant, and other heretical, communities. Although they lack at least some basic means for communion with the People of God, these social bodies are "ecclesial communities."[98]

The characteristics of the "ecclesial community" are described in *Dominus Jesus*. "On the other hand, the ecclesial communities which have not preserved the valid episcopate and the genuine and integral substance of the Eucharistic mystery, are not Churches in the proper sense."[99] This does not mean that members of such a community cannot experience salvation or that they have no positive union with the People of God. Their communion is real, though imperfect, if the individuals are baptized. Their baptism confers grace and the character of conformity to Christ and so is oriented towards full incorporation into the Church.

Those who lack communion, the Orthodox or the Lefebvrites, for example, do not have a defect of faith, but rather a defect of charity. They are in schism and though they lack full communion and the character of their Churches is distinct from the "ecclesial community," the term "Church"[100] can certainly be applied to them. They "possess an episcopate, celebrate the holy Eucharist and cultivate devotion to the Virgin Mother of God."[101] These are the various Eastern Churches, which have preserved all these elements but do not recognize full authority of the primacy of Rome.

This doctrine has been much misunderstood in the time since the Council. The Doctrinal Commission at Vatican II certainly understood the relationship between the ecclesial communities, the separated Churches and the Church in this way. This distinction goes right to the heart of Vatican II.

> Pontifical documents in many places speak about the separated Eastern "Churches." For the Protestants the recent Popes use the term "Christian communities."[102]

The Council had an ecumenical intention, so the Fathers were at pains to underscore the positive. Though both Protestant and Orthodox bodies have an imperfect communion with the Church and their situations are different, this does not mean there is no connection at all. The Fathers were especially solicitous to emphasize that the positive elements found in the Protestant bodies were true social characteristics and were true means to a "certain real connection"[103] with the People of God.

In fact, "the elements of this already-given Church exist, joined together in their fullness in the Catholic Church and, without this fullness, in other communities." "Therefore, these separated Churches and communities as such, though we believe they suffer from defects, have by no means been deprived of significance and importance in the mystery of salvation. For the spirit of Christ has not refrained from using them as a means of salvation which derive their efficacy from the very fullness of grace and truth entrusted to the Catholic Church."

The Council teaches the same doctrine, and the Doctrinal Commission was clear on why the expression "a certain real connection" was used.

Some of the fathers wanted to suppress the term "a certain." Truly sanctifying grace is invoked here, which the Holy Spirit produces by his power in well-disposed non-Catholic christians [*sic*]; "a certain" seems to induce a less pleasing sense. The Commission therefore added "real" to avoid a pejorative interpretation. Yet, the Commission also preserved "a certain" to show that this connection between Protestants and Catholics is not perfect.[105]

The same idea also applies to those who are not Christian. Though they do not have Churches in the proper sense, or even ecclesial bodies, nevertheless, there are some positive elements of union with the People of God through the Natural Law. "Finally, those who have not yet received the Gospel are related to the People of God in various ways."[106]

For many during and after Vatican II, the inclusion of this paragraph in the document seemed truly revolutionary. The whole discussion of the possibility of those outside the Church being related to the Church in various ways seemed like a new idea. In fact, it was an old idea. When St. Thomas examines the necessity of faith in Christ for salvation, he makes the distinction between implicit and explicit faith. According to this distinction, Christ is the head of all men, some who are actually members of the Church and others who are potentially members of the Church. The footnote to the sentence quoted above from *Lumen Gentium*, paragraph 16 cites a text from St. Thomas which says, "Those who are infidels, although they are not members of the Church in act, yet are members of the Church in potency. This potency is founded on two things: first and principally on the power of Christ which is sufficient to save the whole human race and secondarily on free will." [107]

The norms for determining how the members of non-Christian religions can be considered members of the Church follow both of these characteristics. The power of Christ is sufficient to save all men, but to be an actual part of the Church they must have faith in this power. This faith may be implicit, following the norms for free will and invincible ignorance. Classically, there are two norms that express this and must be observed. First, *nulla salus ex Ecclesia* (outside the Church there is no salvation), which expresses the centrality of Christ for salvation. Second, God never condemns those who do what they can. Someone who follows what lights he is able to have about God in his religion can receive grace through the positive things in his religion that are connected to Christianity, provided it is not morally possible for him to know any better.

There is nevertheless one basic article of faith—such a person must believe. "Without faith it is impossible to please God. For whoever would draw near to God must believe that he exists and that he rewards those who seek him." (Hebrews 11:6) Depending on where one fits into the economy of salvation, this basic faith must be more explicit. Like the first principles of a science, the articles of faith are all contained implicitly in this first one. The closer one is to Christ, the more explicit must be the knowledge of him derived from these two premises. "It is possible that according to a diversity of times, the explanation and distinction of these [explicit truths of faith] increased before the coming of Christ, 'so that the closer people existed to the coming of the Savior, the more fully they should perceive the mysteries of salvation.'" [108]

So one can certainly hold that people who are non-Christians can be related to the People of God, but they must have faith, however implicit, to be actually members. Others are members only in potency. This is very far from the "anonymous Christian" idea of Karl Rahner, S.J., [109] who holds that there are those who are actually members of the Church, though anonymously. These would be in potency, but not in act. Their faith may be implicit, but it cannot be just in anything. They must objectively believe certain things about God. One could not deny the existence of God and be an anonymous Christian because one would be denying the most basic article of faith which implicitly contains all the rest.

Those who are members *in voto Ecclesiae* are primarily the catechumens. These could include members of other religions, but again the principle of invincible ignorance and the positive channels of union with the Church would have been emphasized, in which case, these people would make as positive and explicit act of faith as their lights allow.

> Those who, through no fault of their own, do not know the Gospel of Christ or his Church, but who nevertheless seek God with a sincere heart and, moved by grace, try in their actions to do his will as they know it through the dictates of their conscience —those too may achieve eternal salvation. Nor will divine providence deny the assistance necessary for salvation to those who, without any fault of theirs, [invincible ignorance] have not yet arrived at an explicit knowledge of God, and who, not without grace, strive to lead a good life.[110]

In paragraph 16 *Lumen Gentium* takes up the question of the positive channels of union through which such an implicit faith could bring about salvation.

The Jews certainly have the Old Covenant, and others natural reason to teach them. Pope John Paul II examines both the positive aids and the negative influences of all these religions in his book, *Crossing the Threshold of Hope.*[111] Regarding the various world religions, the Pope discusses their positive elements with great respect. "The words of the Council recall the conviction, long rooted in the Tradition, of the existence of the so-called *semina Verbi* (seeds of the Word), present in all religions."[112] However, the Pope also expresses grave reservations about some of their most characteristic tenets.

Of Buddhism, though it involves the search for eternity which characterizes all religions, the Pontiff writes, "Between Christianity and the religions of the Far East, in particular Buddhism, there is an essentially different way of perceiving the world."[113] God is basically regarded as impersonal in Buddhism and as identified with the world. Of Islam, despite a common belief in one God and the fact that "some of the most beautiful names in the human language are given to the God of the Koran [...] he is ultimately a God outside of the world, a God who is only majesty, never Emmanuel, God-with-us. Islam is not a religion of redemption."[114] Though the Pope roundly condemns anti-Semitism and extols the common heritage of the Old Testament between Christians and Jews, it is a fact that the Jews do not accept the New Testament. The Pope hopes "the time will come when the people of the Old Covenant will be able to see themselves as part of the New Covenant."[115] When this will be must be left to the Holy Spirit. In the meantime, Judaism has certainly the most powerful and obvious link with the People of God in Catholicism.

Though all these religious elements do not constitute union with the People of God, they must be regarded as a preparation for the Gospel, some remote, some proximate.

> According to the ancient Fathers, certain religious elements can pre-exist the Gospel and be considered as a divinely given preparation. These are the *seeds of truth* (italics original), namely the notions about God and the soul and certain "universal explanations" (*rationes*) about which St. Justin, Tertullian and Origen treat.[116]

The existence of these elements does not excuse the Church from missionary effort, but spurs her on because she realizes that all these elements naturally belong in union with her. Though accepting positive Gospel preparations in all cultures, the Church must "purify, raise up and perfect"[117] these rites and customs to use them as a fit vehicle of union with the People of God here on earth but, more especially, in heaven. The whole world is not *ipso facto* a member of Christ, but is invited to be so and must become so.

At the end of this treatment of missionary activity, the three great images for the Church used by Vatican II round out chapter 2: the People of God, the Mystical Body of Christ and the Temple of the Holy Spirit, which will be important in the second half of the Constitution. It is important to notice that these three images are used in conjunction with each other. It would be completely inadequate to emphasize one, say the People of God, at the expense of the others. All three must be affirmed and rest together, as do the Persons of the Trinity whom they represent. The People of God are in communion with all Three Persons; the missionary effort of the Church thus has a Trinitarian dimension.

CHAPTER FOUR
The Mystical Body of Christ I
The Hierarchy

The Divine Source of Authority in the People of God

Perhaps no question in the Church is more debated than the hierarchy. Many believe that Vatican II denied papal infallibility taught in Vatican I, and established a kind of federation of individual Churches around the local bishops, much like the World Council of Churches. In fact, the Church has never thought of herself in this way. "The universal Church cannot be conceived as the sum of particular Churches, or as a federation of particular Churches."[118]

The People of God is a true society, but one that is different than any ordinary human society. "Clearly the relationship between the universal Church and the particular Churches is a mystery and cannot be compared to that which exists between the whole and its parts in a purely human group or society."[119] The next logical question becomes an examination of the hierarchical nature of the Church. Once the character of the society of the Church has been delineated *vis-à-vis* other religions, then the nature of the inner structure of the Church must be delineated. In the last two chapters, I made the point that the People of God is not the sole image of the Church but must be completed by the images of the Mystical Body of Christ and the Temple of the Holy Spirit. These images are addressed in the rest of *Lumen Gentium*. The Mystical Body of Christ is specified in all its various forms and offices in chapter 3 on the hierarchy, and chapter 4 on the laity. The Temple of the Holy Spirit is examined in the remaining four chapters under the aspect of the Act of the Church, which completes its Being. This Act is the holiness of the members, the reason the structure of the Church exists.

Since the Church is a supernatural society, Christ must divinely institute it. Since it is based on a communion of life between the Father, Son and Holy Spirit, the authority of the Church must reflect this communion of life and be divinely instituted itself. The nature of that authority must necessarily differ from that of a merely human society; it must be a hierarchy of the service of grace in the members.

> [This is] the communion (*communio, koinonia*) of the People of God as it is fostered in the Church by the vocation and ministry of the bishops, which are likewise a form of service (*diakonia*) to the community. It is significant that the Council Fathers placed the chapter on the hierarchy immediately after the chapter on the People of God, so as to bring out the fact of the organic link between them.[120]

Vatican II was not interested in the question of papal authority, as that had already been defined at Vatican I.

> This teaching concerning the institution, the permanence, the nature and import of the sacred primacy of the Roman Pontiff and his infallible teaching office, the sacred synod proposes anew to be firmly believed by the faithful [...][121]

But Vatican I had meant to take up the question of the bishops and the laity among many other schema; it simply did not have the time because of the political situation in Rome at the time. Of course, the two questions are related and require two concepts, which the Council stressed and which have been emphasized ever since: communion and collegiality.

The College of Bishop—Origin and Nature

Since Vatican II, many have taken the term "collegiality" to refer to a parliamentary democracy, meant to apply to all levels of authority in the Church, from the episcopacy to religious life or parish councils. Clarification of the term, thus, is warranted.

Vatican II makes clear, with all the tradition of the Church, that "Christ the Lord set up in his Church a variety of offices which aim at the good of the whole body."[122] He endowed the holders of these offices with "sacred power."[123] These are the bishops who are to serve the communion of the members of the Church, with the Holy Trinity, in grace. Bishops must be one and undivided, as are the persons of the Trinity. Vatican II in union with Vatican I proclaims that "he [Christ] put Peter at the head of the other apostles, and in him he set up a lasting and visible source and foundation of the unity both of faith and communion."[124] Vatican II now "proposes to publicly proclaim and enunciate clearly the doctrine concerning the bishops, successors of the apostles, who together with Peter's successor, the Vicar of Christ and the visible head of the whole Church, direct the house of the living God."[125]

The nature of the episcopal college is based on the communion which the Church enjoys as a society with the Trinity. "At the heart of the Church's self-understanding is the notion of *communio*: primarily, *a sharing through grace in the life of the Father given us through Christ and in the Holy Spirit.*"[126] "[T]he ecclesiology of communion is the central and fundamental idea of the Council's documents."[127] The foundation of the social character of the Church is not just the union of wills acting in common under the direction of a human intellect, as is the case with societies based on human, or even natural, law. The social character of the Church is based on a supernatural addition to the soul of the Christian, given in Baptism. This supernatural addition is the habitual gift of sanctifying grace, which is a true change in the person, and the character of conformity to Christ. The reception of grace involves a true change in the soul.

The social character of the Church reflects this. Authority is exercised in the Church not according to a merely horizontal dimension, like ordinary earthly authority, which would suffice if reason were sufficient to know all the truths necessary to pursue the purpose of the society of the Church. In fact, after the Original Sin reason is deficient in knowing even those truths necessary for the acquired human virtues which human beings are capable of by nature. Reason is even more deficient in knowing those supernatural truths that have their origin in the communion with the Trinity and which necessarily demand faith so men may hold them with certainty. This communion truly involves "partaking in divine nature." (2 Peter 1:4) The vertical dimension of unity with God in grace, founded on the supernatural knowledge of faith and the supernatural love of charity, is essential to support the horizontal dimension. In fact, it is both the principle (efficient cause) and purpose (final cause) for the existence and action of the society of the Church. "[C]ommunion always involves a double dimension: the *vertical* (communion with God) and the *horizontal* (communion among men)."[128]

The communion with God is not only vertical and horizontal, but also invisible and visible. "The link between the invisible and visible elements of ecclesial communion constitutes the Church as a sacrament of salvation."[129] The primary sign of the visible communion is the college of bishops. Each bishop heads a particular Church, which has the relation of communion or "mutual interiority."[130]

The bishops of these particular Churches form a permanent body, which is the permanent successor, the college of the Apostles. "[Christ] constituted them [the apostles] in the form of a permanent assembly, at the head of which he placed Peter."[131] The Doctrinal Commission at Vatican II knew that the term "college" might be misunderstood, as use of this term might seem to suggest a shift from a hierarchical structure of the Church to a parliamentary structure in which all the bishops might be considered *primus inter pares*. Further, theologians might begin to justify looking at the Church as a democracy after the model of the modern constitutional state. This in turn might influence the way authority is exercised in all the different ministries of the Church, including religious life. Pastors might begin to reject the interventions of higher authorities, and bishops and national conferences might begin to reject the authority of Rome.

The commission wished to make abundantly clear that the use of the term "college" had nothing to do with ideas about parliamentary democracy. "The name 'college' is not understood in the juridical sense about an assembly of perfect equals; but of a stable assembly, instituted by the Lord."[132] In other words, the term "college" does not express an equal power of the assembly of bishops with the Pope, but merely defines the nature of the apostolic succession, i.e. that the Pope and bishops are truly the successors of the Apostles.

Collegiality, then, does not refer to a parliamentary democracy, but simply affirms that the authority given to Peter and the Apostles with respect to the unity of the Word and sacraments is also enjoyed by the Pope and bishops, who are their successors. This authority is enjoyed because they have a unique role to fill in the communion of the Church—the unity of doctrine and practice of the faith in both the whole Church and the individual diocese.

By the end of the Council Paul VI was very solicitous to clarify the term "college," because misunderstandings had already begun to multiply—so much so that an explanatory note (*nota praevia*) was added at the end of *Lumen Gentium*. This note explains very clearly that "college" "is not to be taken in the *strictly juridical* sense, that is, as a group of equals who transfer their powers to their chairman, but as a permanent body whose form and authority is to be ascertained from revelation."[133] The Explanatory Note is even more precise on this point, lest there be any question. "In other words, it [the college] is not a distinction between the Roman Pontiff and the bishops taken together but between the Roman Pontiff by himself and the Roman Pontiff along with the bishops."[134]

In paragraph 20, the Fathers of the Council also explain the concept of collegiality on the basis of apostolic succession. The Doctrinal Commission clarified that the fact of such a succession is clear from as early as Clement of Rome (third pontiff after St. Peter) and generally hinted at in Scripture, though the "scriptural indications are clarified in Tradition."[135] This succession is the foundation of the *munus* (office) of the bishops, who, surrounded by the priests and deacons, preside over the Church as pastors. St. Ignatius of Antioch and other ancient Fathers describe the purpose of this office as "doctrine, worship and government."[136] The Fathers at Vatican II did not specifically consider certain debated questions, such as whether Peter and the Apostles could pass on personal prerogatives (such as being the founders of Churches) to the Apostles, but explicitly established only that the office (*munus*) of the Apostles is to pastor the Church.[137]

Vatican I had exhaustively examined the nature of the authority of the Pope. Employing the traditional understanding of apostolic succession, Vatican II clarified the nature of the authority received by the bishops. It is a "signal service" (*eximium*).[138] This word was used by the Fathers of the Council to underline that episcopal authority is an "action of Christ."[139] The action is one of fatherly care in which the bishops serve the orders of truth and grace by the power of Christ.

The episcopal office has its origin in a unity of being that is supernatural, so a bishop is not a mere papal legate. Since his office involves supernatural life and is instituted by Christ, he enjoys the power that office confers directly from the sacrament of episcopal consecration.

> ... [T]hey [the Apostles] passed on to their auxiliaries the gift of the Spirit, which is transmitted down to our day through episcopal consecration. The

> sacred synod teaches, moreover, that the fullness of
> the sacrament of Orders is conferred by episcopal
> consecration.[140]

The character of the sacrament of Orders, which is conferred in
its fullness in the sacrament of episcopal ordination, is the source of
the power of the bishop in his role of guiding the flock, as it is also
the source of the power of the priest to consecrate and forgive sins,
and of the deacon to pursue his ministry of service. The bishops have
this power on their own and not as delegates of the Pope.

> A man becomes a member of the college in virtue of
> episcopal consecration and hierarchical communion
> with the head of the college and its members.[141]

> It is the unmistakable teaching of tradition, that an
> ontological share in the sacred functions is given by
> consecration.[142]

This is because the character of Orders is a true ontological change
in the soul of the person on whom it is conferred, allowing that person
to perform certain actions and give certain commands which no one
else in the Church can. This is a supernatural change and is ordered to
a supernatural action. When they receive this character, the bishops,
"in a resplendent and visible manner, take the place of Christ himself,
teacher, shepherd, and priest, and act in his person."[143]

Bishops exercise their office by virtue of this ordination, to teach
doctrine (prophet), to govern with charity (king) and to sanctify by
offering the sacrifice of Christ (priest). Though they have this power
ontologically in their own right from the sacrament of Holy Orders
and not as papal appointees, they cannot exercise that power apart
from the other bishops in the college, and especially not apart from
the head, the Pope. Communion and collegiality go together. Communion in being demands collegiality in act.

The College of Bishops—Unity in Acting

The fact of the existence of the college in act is shown in many
ways. One is that the very sacrament by which bishops are ordained
to the episcopacy is usually conferred by more than one bishop.
The ecumenical council is another. Since the ontological power is
conferred in a collegial way, then it must be exercised in this way;
action follows being.

Episcopal collegiality is expressed in two ways. Pope John Paul expresses this well.

> Our own relationship of ecclesial communion—*col-legialitas effectiva ET affectiva*—is discovered in the same mystery of the Church. [...] In this perspective too, we must see the ministry of the Successor of Peter, not only as a "global service," reaching each particular Church from "outside" as it were, but *as belonging already to the essence of each particular Church from "within."* Precisely because this rela-tionship of ecclesial communion—our *collegialitas effectiva et affectiva*—is such an intimate part of the structure of the Church's life, its exercise calls for each and every one of us to be completely one in mind and heart with the will of Christ regarding our different roles in the college of Bishops.[144]

These two collegialities are the union in profession of faith, unity of sacraments and ecclesial government (*collegialitas effectiva*), and charity (*collegialitas affectiva*). Heresy is a sin against the first expres-sion of communion, and schism against the second.

All acts of the college must include the Pope, who is the head of the college. This relationship has a biblical origin, mirroring the relation of Peter to the Apostles. "From the desire of the Supreme Pontiff the question was asked of the Pontifical Biblical Commission as to whether [...] St. Peter and the rest of the Apostles can be said to constitute an apostolic college. The response of the Biblical Com-mission is positive."[145] Nevertheless, this means that in the acts of the college, though bishops enjoy jurisdiction and the right to teach doctrine and guide the liturgy in their individual dioceses, their rights and authority are limited by the confines of the diocese. "Individual bishops, in so far as they are set over particular Churches, exercise their pastoral office over the portion of the People of God assigned to them, not over other Churches nor the Church universal."[146] Only the Pope as an individual bishop enjoys these rights over the whole Church.

Any good ecclesiology must recognize that the college of bish-ops does not detract from the authority of the Pope. The teaching of Vatican I remains intact: "[The Pope has] full, supreme and universal power over the whole Church, a power that he can always exercise unhindered."[147] The bishops depend on the Pope to act collegially, and this is especially the case in an ecumenical council because "[t]here is never an ecumenical council which is not confirmed or at least recognized as such by Peter's successor."[148]

The authority of the college is also "supreme and full."[149] Since this is a collegial authority, and the Pope is the head of the college, the bishops can never act with this authority, even in their individual dioceses, apart from the Pope. He is present, confirming them in doctrine whenever they speak, because they always speak in union with the college if they speak according to their office. "Together with the head, the Supreme Pontiff, and never apart from him, they have supreme and full authority over the universal Church."[150]

Even if all the bishops of the world were to agree on something, and the Pope were to disagree, the bishops' act would not be a collegial act and therefore would only be private opinion, not binding on the consciences of the faithful. "The college or body of bishops has for all that no authority unless united with the Roman Pontiff, Peter's successor, as its head [...]."[151]

Though individual bishops exercise no jurisdiction (*etiamsi per actum iurisdictionis non exerceatur*)[152] over the rest of the Church, they are still bound by the communion at the basis of collegiality not to limit their interest and action merely to the Church over which they exercise jurisdiction. They act according to this care for the whole Body of Christ in the missions, in the particular Churches founded in the East around the patriarchal sees, and also in episcopal conferences.

Episcopal conferences are an especially practical way of demonstrating the collegiality of the Church. However, a few important points must be kept in mind, and the Congregation of the Doctrine of the Faith clarified these points in the Apostolic Letter *Apostolos Suos* in 1998.

The first is that the episcopal conference is an important pastoral implementation of the collegial spirit of Vatican II. Canonically, these conferences are not viewed in the post-Vatican II Church as a merely incidental part of Church life.

Episcopal conferences constitute a concrete application of the collegial spirit. Basing itself on the prescriptions of the Second Vatican Council, the Code of Canon Law gives a precise description: 'The conference of bishops, a permanent institution, is a grouping of bishops of a given country or territory whereby, according to the norm of law, they jointly exercise certain pastoral functions on behalf of the Christian faithful of their territory' [...][153]

Secondly, though episcopal conferences are a necessary part of the governing of the Church, their primary responsibility is pastoral. In themselves, they are not instituted by Christ, as are the papacy and the episcopal college. Though a practical exercise of the collegial spirit, they do not enjoy a jurisdiction to teach doctrine that is equivalent in any sense to the Pope's or to the college as a whole. "Nonetheless, this territorially based exercise of the episcopal ministry never takes on the collegial nature proper to the actions of the order of bishops as such, which alone holds the supreme power over the whole Church."[154]

Thirdly, the episcopal conference of a region is a marvelous way of emphasizing the responsibility and care that each bishop has for the whole Church, but in itself it has no *munus docendi* (office of teaching), no *munus regendi* (power of ruling) and no *munus sanctificandi* (power of sanctifying). Since the Catholic Church is a society that reflects one Trinity and one Christ, it cannot be a loose composition of churches like the World Council of Churches, each based on national or regional forms. "'[T]he universal Church cannot be conceived as the sum of the particular Churches, or as a federation of particular Churches.'"[155]

Lastly, if the episcopal conference does exercise jurisdiction in some matter, this is due not to the conference itself, but to the power delegated by the Holy See, which represents the college of bishops. The Pope is the head of the college, so he can delegate this power to some local body. The diocesan bishop and the papacy have this power by divine institution as an extension of Christ's power. The college of bishops has this power by divine institution also, as Christ founded the college when he established Peter and the college of the Apostles. The episcopal conference has no such authority in itself because it is not of divine institution. Only human delegation invests these bodies with jurisdiction.

> In the episcopal conference the bishops jointly exercise the episcopal ministry for the good of the faithful of the territory of the conference; but for that exercise to be legitimate and binding on individual bishops, there is need for the intervention of the supreme authority of the Church which, through universal law or particular mandates, entrusts determined questions to the deliberation of the episcopal conference. Bishops, whether individually or united in conference, cannot autonomously limit their own sacred power in favor of the episcopal conference, and even less can they do so in favor of one of its parts, whether the permanent council or a commission or the president.[156]

The important point to emphasize here is that the bishops have an authority in their own right in their dioceses. They also have their own authority in a college, which must always include the authority of the Bishop of Rome as the head of the college. National or regional conferences do not enjoy that authority and therefore cannot bind individual bishops, much less the faithful, because, as legislative bodies, they do not have the strength of jurisdiction from Christ. Their jurisdiction must depend on the other bodies giving it to them. There is no resemblance between parliamentary or democratic constitutional government in the binding power of the episcopal conference. Nor are interventions of the Holy See in a country those of an alien government. Since the Holy See invests the conference with authority, the Holy See is present to every decision, at least by recognizing it.

> The *recognitio* of the Holy See serves furthermore to guarantee that, in dealing with new questions posed by the accelerated social and cultural changes characteristic of present times, the doctrinal response will favor communion and not harm it, and will rather prepare an eventual intervention of the universal magisterium.[157]

The College of Bishops (munus docendi)

As we have seen, the Second Vatican Council seriously examined the question of the nature of the episcopacy because this question was to have been treated in Vatican I, but was abandoned because the Fathers were forced by the political situation in Rome to leave the Council without treating many of the proposed topics. Since the topic they did treat was the nature of the papal infallibility, some had the idea that the Pope was the source of authority in the Church and the bishops simply his legates. This is not true. To understand the teaching on the episcopacy reflected in Vatican II, one must understand exactly what was being defined at Vatican I.

The Relatio *of Bishop Vincent Gasser*

The First Vatican Council addressed the authority of the papacy at great length. The Second Vatican Council reaffirmed that teaching without questioning the nature of the infallibility of the Pope, but to understand how collegiality in teaching was addressed in Vatican II one must examine precisely what Vatican I defined.

The historical climate of Europe surrounding the definition of the infallibility was conditioned by the heresy of Gallicanism. According to this heresy, the teachings of the Pope were not sufficient to clarify Catholic practice in faith and morals without the posterior approval of the bishops of a given country, and perhaps even of the king. The source of the term "Gallicanism" was the Declaration of the French Clergy made in March 1682 at the behest of Louis XIV. "This Declaration [...] held that the Pope has the chief role when it comes to matters of faith, but that, nonetheless, his decisions needed confirmation by the judgement of the entire Church."[158] The Church was also attacked by the rationalists of the nineteenth century who thought there was no higher truth than human reason, and so no society based on grace and revelation above the state. Religion, thus, was reduced to sentiment.

Against this background, the bishops at Vatican I wanted to declare the necessity of Revelation for the fullness of human truth, and the unique character of the society based on this Revelation. They wanted to clarify the fact that the Church was the society founded by this Revelation and in which this Revelation is known definitively. This was the point of the declaration of the infallibility of the Pope: the bishops wanted to teach clearly that the Church was not the state, but was a society founded on a higher reason: God's reason brought to us in Revelation, specifically the Revelation taught by Christ. As this was the case, models used for authority in the state, a society founded on human reason were insufficient to explain the nature of authority in the Church. The teaching on the infallibility of the Pope was based on this intention, and the bishops meant to deny that any posterior approval was necessary for a teaching of the Pope to define truly a doctrine taught by Christ.

In his *relatio* given at the end of the session of the Council that approved the infallibility of the Pope, Bishop Vincent Ferrer Gasser [1809-1879] sought to clarify just what was taught by the Council and what was not. Bishop Gasser was the prince-bishop of Brixen. As a bishop he was an example of asceticism and a great scholar. He was one of the outstanding theologians at Vatican I.

> [H]e was responsible for having inserted into the schema [on papal infallibility] the explanation that the papal primacy does not limit the ordinary and immediate governing authority of the bishops, but protects and strengthens it. Finally (July 11, 1870), he presented to the Council fathers the decree, composed by himself, on papal infallibility in a four hour Latin speech with such conviction that the decree was approved by a majority of the bishops with only minor changes, and was solemnly defined a week later.[159]

This *relatio* was accepted by the Council Fathers as the authentic interpretation of their teaching on infallibility.[160]

First, Bishop Gasser maintains that "absolute infallibility belongs to God alone; he is the first and essential truth, and every other infallibility is communicated to a certain end and has therefore certain limits and conditions."[161] Infallibility is identified as a charismatic grace given to St. Peter and his successors so that they may not err in defining what the Church has always taught. "The *causa efficiens* and *formalis* (efficient and formal cause) is [*sic*] therefore the assistance of the Holy Spirit."[162] This assistance is not the same as biblical inspiration or private revelation, given to individuals under very special circumstances. Infallibility is connected to the office of the papacy, and is not given for an individual purpose or to only a few individuals in history.

Gasser makes an important distinction between a permanent quality in the person of the Pope, and an aid that is personally given to the Pope only in the act of defining *ex cathedra*, i.e. an assurance that his teachings are preserved from error only in the act of defining a doctrine. The title of the document proclaiming the infallibility was changed from simply *The Infallibility of the Roman Pontiff* to *The Infallible Magisterium of the Roman Pontiff* (*De romani pontificis infallibili magisterio*) to avoid the misunderstanding that infallibility was a permanent quality of the Pope himself.

There was an opinion in the Middle Ages that the infallibility resided in the Pope as a unique source (*fontaliter*) and was communicated to the Church through him. Gasser specifically denies this. Though the Pope must approve decrees of councils for them to be acts of the college of bishops, this does not mean that the Pope is the source of the infallibility of the Church. Christ rather promised infallibility to the whole Church, which includes the apostolic college always with Peter and not apart from him, and the theologians after Trent always affirmed that the whole Church was infallible in believing (*in credendo*) when the faithful all unanimously professed a truth.

In his *relatio*, Gasser emphasizes that there is only one infallibility. "This special infallibility of the Roman pontiff is due above all to the Church." (*Haec specialis Romani pontificis infallibilitas ecclesiae opprime convenit ...*) In teaching, this one infallibility has two subjects or material causes: either the Pope teaching a doctrine alone or the college of bishops teaching together with him. "The true reason why the bishops, even gathered in general council, are not infallible in matters of faith and morals without the Pope, is to be found in the fact that Christ promised this infallibility to the whole Magisterium (*in universo magisterio*) of the Church [...]."[163] "In this definition we treat 1) the subject of infallibility, namely the Roman Pontiff as Pontiff, i.e. as a public person in relation to the Universal Church."[164]

The Pope exercises full and supreme power in a personal act when he defines a doctrine. This same full and supreme power is also exercised in the collective act of the whole college as a collective subject, which includes the Pope as the head. The whole Church is the subject of the infallibility in believing by an aid of the Holy Spirit, but acts in two specific organs to define what all believe: one, bishops with Pope; two, the Pope alone. Vatican I defined the nature of the latter; Vatican II formally took up the former, though it stopped short of a *de fide* definition, as there are no new doctrines defined by Vatican II.

Gasser explains that the word "define" must be taken in a strictly theological sense, as "to give a definitive judgement." The Pope must manifest his intention to make a judgement about doctrine. This does not mean simply to bring a controversy to an end, nor does it mean that the judgements of the Pope are without appeal. Gasser means to say that these judgements are true.

In *Pastor Aeternus*, the decree on the infallibility of the papal magisterium, Vatican I says that such definitive teachings are by nature irreformable (*ex sese irreformabiles*). The Gallicans held that such teachings could be considered true only after the rest of the Church consented, which places the weight of the power to define on the approval of the Church as a whole, and suggests liberal democracy or conciliarism.

To do away with any justification to return to Gallicanism, the Fathers at Vatican I added that papal definitions were in themselves (*ex sese*) irreformable and not from consent of the Church. They wanted to emphasize the unique character of theological knowledge. "The exact meaning of the *ex sese* however is: the decision needs no further approval or sanction by the bishops as an act of a parliamentary ratification. The formal reason of infallibility is the divine assistance and no other instance of the Church."[165]

Though the consent of the Church is not needed, the assent of the Church (*assensus ecclesiae*) is never absent because there is a complete connection between the head of the college, the body of the college, and the Church as a whole. The Pope does not have to initiate all doctrinal and moral matters, but unless he agrees to consider them they have no collegial nature because the body cannot act apart from the head, though the head can act personally, and this includes the action of the body.

Many of the Fathers at Vatican I tried to introduce conditions into the definition of papal infallibility. The most famous condition normally required for a papal teaching to be true in the history of theology was expressed: Thus the Pope is infallible when he does what he can (*papa faciens quod est in se est infallibilitas*). This means that the Pope must study the problem and consult with the bishops and with experts. The Fathers at Vatican I thought that this smacked too much of latent Gallicanism. Gasser nuances the argument explaining that the Pope cannot be bound to do what he can or to consult with others because these two conditions pertain to his conscience in the moral order and are between him and God. Interior moral conditions, therefore, cannot be made a part of a dogmatic definition. A charismatic grace like infallibility cannot depend on the Pope's conscience, which is a private affair, but on the Pope's public office within the universal Church.[166]

Other difficulties turned around the use of terms like "absolute," "personal" and "separate" to describe papal infallibility. Gasser answers that infallibility are not said to be "separate" in the sense that the Pope is infallible apart from the consent of the Church or that *de facto* he should not seek means to discern the truth. His infallibility is that of the whole Church. The consent of the Church is a part of his infallibility, but not a condition *de iure* for the action of the Holy Spirit. Gasser says that infallibility is not absolute because this is found in God alone. It is conditioned by subject (the Pope); by object (a solemn definition of faith and morals); and by cause (the action of the Holy Spirit). Some wanted to limit the Pope to a form, but Gasser boldly declares, "Already thousands and thousands of dogmatic judgements have gone forth from the Apostolic See; where is the law that prescribed the form to be observed in such judgements?"[167] Finally, the infallibility is personal, to exclude the distinction made by the Gallicans between the office of Pope and the one who holds the office. In fact, the two are the same. This does not mean that the Pope receives the charism of infallibility as a private person, but rather as a public person in his role as head of the Church.

The Office of Teaching (munus docendi) of the Bishops

Paragraph 25 is a pivotal paragraph in *Lumen Gentium*. The Doctrinal Commission was very clear on the subject matter of this paragraph. "The same infallibility is also acknowledged for the Body of the Bishops, when it produces a definition together with the Roman Pontiff. This pertains to the special and direct object of this paragraph."[168] The Council of Trent taught that teaching was the special office of the bishop (*praecipuum Episcoporum munus*).[169] Vatican II now addresses the special nature of the infallibility of this teaching office in the college of bishops.

Bishop Gasser had taken up the question of the infallibility of the body of the bishops in teaching, but this had not been formally addressed by Vatican I because of the political situation. Vatican I rather defined the extraordinary infallibility of the papal magisterium because the Fathers were preoccupied with the error of Gallicanism. Vatican II clearly affirmed the doctrine of Vatican I concerning the papal magisterium and then went further in developing the subject of the episcopal magisterium. "The infallibility with which Christ willed the Church to be instructed has been utterly identified with the infallibility of the teaching Church; and in fact: either of the whole Episcopacy or of the Roman Pontiff alone."[170] Here one can see the distinction in the material cause or subjects of the infallibility invoked already by Gasser in Vatican I.

It should be clear that the Fathers at Vatican II did not intend to modify in any way the doctrine defined by Vatican I concerning the extraordinary papal magisterium. They did wish to clarify the connection between papal definitions and the college of bishops as a whole, as well as the fact that such definitions are irreformable in themselves.

To anticipate any interpretation of the infallibility that could suggest that the Pope as a private person was infallible in any pronouncement on any matter, *Lumen Gentium* clarifies: "The Roman Pontiff, head of the college of bishops, enjoys this infallibility in virtue of his office, when, as supreme pastor and teacher of all the faithful—who confirms his brethren in faith—he proclaims in an absolute decision a doctrine pertaining to faith or morals."[171] His definitions are irreformable in themselves and not from the assent of the Church, again to preclude Gallicanism and Conciliarism and because they are guaranteed by the charismatic grace of the Holy Spirit. This is the basic doctrine of Vatican I.

The college of bishops is also invested with such a gift in its pronouncements when it speaks as a whole body which includes the head, the Pope. "The infallibility promised to the Church is also present in the body of bishops when, together with the Peter's successor, they exercise the supreme teaching office."[172] The supreme teachings of the Magisterium are not made apart from Revelation. There can be no new public revelation. Revelation is communicated by the twin vehicles of Scripture (revelation in writing) and Tradition (revelation in oral teaching). The Magisterium, whether of the Pope alone or of the bishops together with him, is the servant of Revelation. The Pope and bishops serve to guard and interpret Revelation. Their guardianship demands an aid from God and this takes the form of infallibility. *Ex cathedra* statements and the teachings of ecumenical councils are examples. These would also be an example—but only one kind of example—of the extraordinary Magisterium.

A recent Doctrinal Commentary by Cardinal Ratzinger on the Profession of Faith now required for those who teach in the Church lists three distinctions in the exercise of the teaching of the Magisterium. The first distinction is both the extraordinary Magisterium and the ordinary Magisterium teaching in a solemn manner taken together.

> These doctrines are *contained in the word of God, written or handed down and defined with a solemn judgment as divinely revealed truths either by the Roman Pontiff when he speaks "ex cathedra" or by the college of bishops gathered in council, or infallibly proposed for belief by the ordinary and universal magisterium.*[173]

Examples of this are:

> [...] the articles of faith of the Creed, the various Christological dogmas and the Marian dogmas; the doctrine of the institution of the sacraments by Christ and their efficacy with regard to grace; the doctrine of the real and substantial presence of Christ in the Eucharist and the sacrificial nature of the Eucharistic celebration; the foundation of the Church by the will of Christ; the doctrine on the primacy and the infallibility of the Roman Pontiff; the doctrine on the existence of original sin; the doctrine of the immortality of the soul and on the immediate recompense after death; the absence of error in inspired sacred texts; the doctrine of the grave immorality of the direct and voluntary killing of an innocent human being.[174]

The assent which is required for this type of declaration is "theological faith," a lack of which is punished by a censure of "heresy."[175]

Lumen Gentium speaks of this kind of authoritative teaching in paragraph 25, where the teaching of Vatican I, which applies this to the Pope, is then expanded to include the college of bishops. Indeed, this is the purpose of the decree in Vatican II. The Doctrinal Commission clearly states that:

> The infallibility with which Christ willed his Church be instructed is absolutely (*prorsus*) identified with the infallibility of the teaching Church; and in fact (*quidem*): either of the whole episcopate or uniquely (*singulariter*) of the Roman Pontiff.[176]

Vatican II, therefore, did not change this manner of teaching doctrine in any way. What the Council did address was the question of the relation of the bishops' magisterium to this extraordinary Magisterium. In fact, this relation is dealt with in the second and third distinction made by Cardinal Ratzinger, which reflects the innovative teaching of Vatican II on this matter.

The second distinction respects a further distinction in the ordinary Magisterium. The formula in the profession of faith on which Ratzinger comments is, "I also firmly accept and hold each and everything definitively proposed by the Church regarding teaching on faith and morals." Notice that in relation to the doctrines in the first distinction, these are "definitively taught" but not taught "in a solemn manner."

> The object taught by this formula includes all those teachings belonging to the dogmatic or moral area, which are necessary for faithfully keeping and expounding the deposit of faith, even if they have not been proposed by the Magisterium of the Church as formally revealed.[177]

The assent demanded by these teachings is not one that falls directly under the virtue of faith, but an assent which is "firm and definitive."[178] A person who did not assent to these teachings "would no longer be in full communion with the Catholic Church."[179]

Examples of this sort of teaching are those connected "by logical necessity"[180] with Revelation. This necessity can also be an historical necessity. Some concrete examples are:

> [...] the development in the understanding of the doctrine connected with the definition of papal infallibility, prior to the dogmatic definition of the First

Vatican Council. [...] the doctrine that priestly ordination is reserved only to men. [...] the illicitness of
euthanasia [...] the illicitness of prostitution and of
fornication [...] the legitimacy of the election of the
Roman Pontiff or the celebration of an ecumenical
council, the canonization of saints (dogmatic facts),
the declaration [...] on the invalidity of Anglican
ordinations [...][181]

It would seem that *Humanae Vitae* and the teaching on birth
control could be added to this, because this teaching involves a conclusion of logical necessity on the data of revelation concerning sexual
ethics, even though contraception is never specifically mentioned in
Scripture. This is because Scripture includes in its moral teaching all
that is contained in the Natural Law. Here the true relation between
reason and faith is very evident, as is clear in many of the reflections
of Pope John Paul II on sexual ethics.

Both sorts of teaching—namely, that which is divinely revealed,
and that which is held definitively by logical connection to what is
divinely revealed—are taught infallibly. In the case of the second
kind of doctrine, one held definitively in a non-defining act by the
ordinary and universal Magisterium of bishops, "such a doctrine
can be confirmed or reaffirmed by the Roman Pontiff, even without
recourse to a solemn definition."[182] *Ex cathedra* infallibility spoken of
by Vatican I described a solemn definition by a Pope alone. However,
Vatican I did not limit the infallibility of the Church to teach doctrine
to this one act. This act was merely a special instance of the action
of the Holy Spirit.

Vatican II addressed the second instance of the action of the Holy
Spirit in *Lumen Gentium*. Though this discussion did not involve a
solemn definition, because Paul VI made it clear that no doctrines
were defined in Vatican II, still this teaching of the Council must
be considered a teaching presented to be held definitively under the
rubric of this second distinction.

> Although the bishops, taken individually, do not
> enjoy the privilege of infallibility, they do, however,
> proclaim infallibly the doctrine of Christ on the
> following conditions: namely, when, even though

dispersed throughout the world but preserving for all that among themselves and with Peter's successor the bond of communion, in their authoritative teaching concerning faith and morals, they are in agreement that a particular teaching is to be held definitively and absolutely.[183]

As the Council points out, this is most clearly seen in an ecumenical Council, but infallible teaching can be presented in less solemn, but nonetheless definitive ways. One is the Pope's special office to speak for the college of bishops, even though he does not intend to make a solemn pronouncement. This would be exemplified in the kinds of teachings placed under distinction two.

In addition to these two kinds of teaching, which are both infallible, there is a third. These are "all those teachings—on faith and morals—presented as true or at least as sure, even if they are not defined by a solemn judgement or proposed as definitive by the ordinary and universal Magisterium."[184] The assent demanded of these teachings would be a "religious submission of will and intellect."[185] Teachings contrary to these truths are certainly erroneous and must not be taught.

As examples of doctrines of this sort, Cardinal Ratzinger quotes *Lumen Gentium* almost verbatim. "[O]ne can point in general to teaching set forth by the authentic ordinary Magisterium in a non-definitive way, which require degrees of adherence differentiated according to the mind and will manifested [...] by the nature of the documents, by the frequent repetition of the same doctrine, or by the tenor of the verbal expression."[186] Such doctrines would be those generally taught in the manner of theological discussions, or, e.g. encyclicals on devotion to the Sacred Heart. These are not definitive teachings, but they still require religious submission of the will and intellect because they are made by a religious authority.

Many Catholics believe that Vatican II claimed less infallibility for the Pope than had previously been the case, perhaps because the Council raised the whole issue of further specification of the authority of the College of Bishops and the very use of the term. In fact, in proclaiming that the same divine assistance of the Holy Spirit is present in the college of bishops in union with the Pope, Vatican II extended the infallibility to include acts of the college and the acts of the Pope when he acts not alone but as head of the college. "The same infallibility is acknowledged also in the Body of Bishops, when together with the Roman Pontiff, it advances a definition. This pertains to the special and direct object of this paragraph (#25 in *Lumen Gentium*)."[187]

Moreover, if he wishes, the Pope as the head of the college can exercise the ordinary infallible Magisterium through the magisterium of the bishops. The head can always act for, and in the name of, the college, even in definitions that are not solemn. He is not then acting on his own, exercising the *ex cathedra* authority of his office, but making a collegial act.

> There is no such thing as the college without its head: it is "*The subject of supreme and entire power* over the whole Church." [...] In other words it is not a distinction between the Roman Pontiff and the bishops taken together but between the Roman Pontiff by himself and the Roman Pontiff along with the bishops. The Pope alone, in fact, being head of the college, is qualified to perform certain actions in which the bishops have no competence whatsoever [...] It is for the Pope, to whom the care of the whole flock has been entrusted, to decide the best manner of implementing this care, either personal or collegiate, in order to meet the changing need of the Church in the course of time. The Roman Pontiff undertakes the regulation, encouragement, and approval of the exercise of collegiality as he sees fit.[188]

The complex teaching of this paragraph touches several important points. 1) The formal reason for the truth of papal doctrine is the assistance given by the Holy Spirit, promised to Peter and his successors when they speak not as private persons, but as public persons who represent the common good of the whole Church. 2) The college of bishops enjoys this same truth when it teaches in communion with the Pope. 3) The assent of the whole Church is present in both acts because both occur as a result of the special grace of the Holy Spirit. 4) The further consent of the faithful or individual bishops is not necessary, as the actions of the Pope alone or the college, in either solemn or ordinary definitions, express the truth of the Holy Spirit and thus express the belief of the faithful. They "bear in themselves the consent of the whole community."[189]

The Office of Sanctifying (munus sanctificandi) of the Bishops

The bishops have complete conformity to Christ the High Priest in his office of offering the sacraments to help all in the Church on their quest to live a holy life. Bishops have the fullness of the sacrament of orders, conferred in episcopal consecration or what is today called ordination. Bishops, therefore, do not have this fullness as papal legates, but rather as those who receive the fullness of the character of conformity to Christ.

This fullness of the sacrament of orders is seen especially in the intimate presence of the bishop to each celebration of the Eucharist. Every celebration in a diocese is carried out in communion with the bishop and, therefore, the bishop regulates it. Individual priests cannot take the responsibility to determine readings, translations and rituals on their own; this must be done in communion with the bishop, who is himself in communion with the rest of the hierarchy. Some members of religious orders claimed immediately after Vatican II that since they were "exempt" religious orders directly under the Holy See (like the Dominicans and Franciscans), this freed them from the authority of the bishop in the celebration of the liturgy. Such an attitude completely ignores the concept of communion which is the basis of the society of the Church and is effectively applied in the solicitude and authority of the local bishop over the celebration of the Eucharist in his diocese. "In current legislation, exemption is mainly restricted to the area of internal governance and is not used as an exclusive criterion for the cessation of the power of governance."[190] "The particular Church especially below the diocese whether it is a parish or is assembled for some other reason, yet should always be considered under dependence on the bishop."[191] As the particular Church depends on the bishop, the responsibility of the bishop extends to all the sacraments, the principal instruments of grace. The responsibility and office of the bishop extends to "prayer, preaching and the administration of the sacraments and especially example."[192] The bishop exercises control over all the sacraments.

Traditionally, Western theology holds that bishops occupy a special state of life which demands certain duties of state corresponding to the grace of office and the character of conformity to Christ specially communicated to them. This means that bishops have a "perpetual obligation to things pertaining to perfection together with a certain solemnity."[193] The perfection which characterizes the bishop's state regards his duty as a shepherd, especially not deserting the flock, but "laying down his life for his sheep." (John 10:15) Deacons and priests do not have the same permanent obligation to watch over the faithful, even in the face of persecution. The characteristic role of the bishop is one of "perfecter" (*perfectores*).[194]

The fortitude with which bishops must defend the laity cannot be implemented if they assume a role more compatible with corporate CEOs than fathers. In other words, a bishop cannot assume the role of a mere functionary in a human community. The communion of the Church, with the Trinity and the special servant character of the episcopal office, demand a way of life that corresponds to a servant of grace. Bishops have a special duty of state, coupled with the grace given them to be examples of holiness and to abstain "from all wrongdoing in their conduct."[195] This includes any attempt to guide the liturgical practice of a diocese contrary to the liturgical practice of the Holy See. For example, the bishop has not the competence to command non-ordained individuals, such as seminarians, to preach a homily at Mass. Not only is this practice contrary to Canon Law, and thus not a collegial act, but it sets up in the subject a hopeless conflict of conscience in which he must deny a more remote, but higher, authority to obey a more proximate and local authority. The signal this sends is that disobedience to Church practice and law (some would say divine law) is not only condoned but fostered by the very souls given the charge to protect it. The signal is also given that collegiality does not extend to matters as central as the proclamation of doctrine.

Moreover, since the bishop is called to a higher state of perfection or holiness, when a bishop commits sin, he is held more accountable. This is because by sinning he seems to hold the graces of his state in contempt and his disobedience could scandalize others by suggesting to them (if not tacitly authorizing) that they disobey legitimate authority. Sadly, history teaches that when bishops undermine the authority of Rome, they undermine their own authority as well. When they undermine the Pope, they a *fortiori* undermine the college of which he is the head.

The Office of Governing (munus regendi) of the Bishops

Of late much has been written on the bishops' power of ruling. Some speculated that after the death of Pope John Paul II there would be a new "democratization of the Roman Church." We should not be surprised, perhaps, that such novel ideas are promulgated by the most innovative means. The magazine *Inside the Vatican* has recently published a draft "Constitution of the Catholic Church" which appeared on the Internet[196] and which some are suggesting is the new form which the Catholic Church must take. It says in part:

d) Pope

1. The Pope of the universal Church shall be elected for a single ten-year term by Delegates selected by the National Councils.

a) The number of Delegates from National Councils to the Papal election shall be proportional to the number of registered Catholics in a nation, to be determined by an appropriate international committee.

b) The Delegates shall be chosen as representatively as possible, one-third being bishops.[197]

One "Italian Vatican expert,"[198] Giancarlo Zizola,[199] now proposes to create a "collegial papacy."[200] The new style of the papacy would have the following characteristics: the reform of the Synod of Bishops; the reform of the nominating process for bishops; direct participation of the laity; autonomy of bishops' conferences; reform of the Roman curia. Each of these "reforms" has the democratization of the Church as its avowed purpose. The reform of the Synod of Bishops is to be carried out by making bishops a kind of senate or congress. The choice of bishops is not to take place in Rome, but the local church is to choose the bishops, as in the early Church. The laity are to be as involved as possible in the decisions of the Church. Further, one must reverse a tendency in the recent Roman documents, which state that episcopal conferences have no *munus docendi* (authority to teach) in themselves, and all bishops in local conferences must make decisions by majority rule.

While a number of these changes are not in themselves compromising to the papacy, it is clear that the general thrust of these reforms, taken together, is to promote a new interpretation of the Church that departs from the traditional Catholic perspective. Zizola states it boldly: "In this perspective the pontificate of John Paul II may be interpreted as the terminal phase of the absolute pontifical monarchy."[201]

Ideas like Zizola's are very prevalent in the Church since Vatican II and often invoke the Council's authority as their justification. Sadly, these notions fly in the face of the Church's whole tradition regarding who has jurisdiction in teaching and governing. *Lumen Gentium*, paragraph 28, now directly addresses the problem of episcopal jurisdiction in regard to ruling *munus regendi*, and this, in turn, will be applied further on in *Lumen Gentium* to the bishops' responsibility for teaching, *munus docendi*.

Lumen Gentium is very clear in its application of the ideas already developed as first principles for the Church as a society, to the way bishops exercise jurisdiction in the Church. The principles developed here presume those explained in previous chapters about the nature of the college of bishops and the manner of exercising collegiality in the Church. Bishops receive their authority to govern from the sacrament of orders, i.e. directly from Christ. They are, therefore, truly "vicars"[202] of Christ in local churches. They are not "vicars of the Roman Pontiff"[203] who receive jurisdiction from the Pope. Their jurisdiction over the local Church in the name of Christ is "proper, ordinary and immediate."[204] The authority of the bishop over the liturgy was explained in the last section; now this authority is expanded to include every aspect of Church life. The power of governing is an implementation of the bishop's pastoral role and has traditionally included "proposing laws, pronouncing judgment, and administering in various ways."[205]

Though the bishops have a "sacred right and duty"[206] to exercise authority in all these ways, since they are part of a college, with the Pope as its head, in exercising this authority they are "ultimately controlled by the supreme authority of the Church."[207] Therefore, if they were to act irresponsibly against the college in the use of their authority, which they possess directly from Christ, their acts would not be episcopal acts. In other words, they receive the fact of their power to govern from Christ, not from the Church, laity, other clergy, or the Pope. This is because the Church is a supernatural institution, and only Christ can be the author of such supernatural power. But as this power is received in a society which is Christ's Mystical Body, bishops are accountable to this society for its use, whether the college acts as a whole or the Pope acts representing the college. If a bishop teaches a doctrine or implements a practice contrary to the practice or teaching of the universal Church, this act is not a collegial act, and therefore, it is not binding on the faithful.

The bishop is primarily accountable to Christ, as he is truly a minister of Christ's supernatural life of divine grace, truly an embodiment of the Good Shepherd. As a result, he must personally be interested in the life of grace in his diocese. Though the Church has an earthly face, and this entails much interest in things like finances and property, the bishop must avoid at all costs any appearance of transforming his ministry into a mere human corporation. Sadly, some bishops after Vatican II seem distressed that their jurisdiction in their diocese is controlled by Rome on the one hand, and yet on the other they seem willing to hand this jurisdiction over to lay factions or the episcopal conference of the country or experts like psychiatrists and lawyers. In the recent pedophilia crisis, some of the bishops seemed to think that this lay involvement absolved them from further interest in a serious pastoral difficulty in their dioceses. This is a serious misreading of Vatican II. George Weigel characterizes it well:

> In the final analysis, it is really a question of imagination, or self-understanding. And that, for bishops, is an irreducibly theological question. To repeat: A bishop who truly believes that he is what the Catholic Church teaches he is—a successor of the apostles who makes present in the Church today the living headship of Christ the Good Shepherd—does not behave like a corporate executive managing a crisis in which he has little personal involvement.[208]

> A brief reading of Acts should suffice to demonstrate that the apostles were not managers of the local branch offices of an up-and-coming religious organization trying to find its market niche.[209]

If the bishops are not vicars of the Pope, they are also certainly not "vicars of their national conference."[210] In view of the present tendency of some in the Church to invest the synod and the episcopal conference with jurisdiction in their own right, it is important to keep clear that these bodies are a laudable implementation of the very collegiality that was so much on the minds of the Fathers in Vatican II. "Episcopal Conferences constitute a concrete application of the collegial spirit."[211] It is also important to remember that the collegiality already examined in the prior paragraphs was not a parliamentary democracy.

The most recent apostolic letter of Pope John Paul II, *Apostolos Suos*, makes this abundantly clear. The episcopal conference, and, *a fortiori*, the synod, has no jurisdiction in and of itself for the simple reason that, unlike the papacy and the office of bishop, neither was instituted by Christ. If the bishops do not derive their authority from the Pope, they certainly do not derive their authority from each other or from a national Synod. Nor is the constitution of the Church a result of ordinary human factors, like the universal synod. Though each episcopal conference is responsible for itself, "[t]hese must however receive the *recognitio* of the Apostolic See."[212]

> When the Bishops of a territory jointly exercise certain pastoral functions for the good of the faithful, such joint exercise of the episcopal ministry is a concrete application of the collegial spirit *(affectus collegialis)*, which is the soul of the collaboration between the Bishops at the regional, national and international levels.
>
> In fact, the power of the College of Bishops over the whole Church is not the result of the sum of the powers of the individual Bishops over their particular Churches; it is the pre-existing reality in which the individual bishops participate.[213]

Fr. Yves Congar said that the ability of the episcopal conferences to enjoy jurisdiction in teaching was based on three conditions:

> 1) if they were unanimous (in decision);
> 2) after recognition by the Holy See if the decision came from a two-thirds vote;
> 3) when canon law leaves application of some measure to the episcopal conference (e.g., Communion in the mouth or hand).[214]

With the exception of the last condition, *Apostolos Suos* expresses the same truth. Concerning the first condition, if there is not a unanimous decision, the *recognitio* of the Holy See seems to satisfy for this. Thus, the decision of an episcopal conference can bind the conscience to assent if the decision meets these conditions:

> (1) It must be a statement issued by the conference in plenary session; not by its doctrinal commission or executive committee.
> (2) It must be approved either by a unanimous vote of all the members, or by at least two thirds of the members having a deliberative vote.
> (3) If it was not approved unanimously, it cannot be published without first receiving the *recognitio* of the Holy See.[215]

These conditions clearly affirm the points made earlier about the two sources of infallibility and, therefore, collegiality. There is no middle ground between the jurisdiction of the Pope over the whole Church and the jurisdiction of the bishop over his local church. "This would indicate that the binding effect of the acts of an episcopal conference derives from two sources: the universal authority of the Holy See and the local authority of individual bishops."[216]

There can be no question of the universal synod occupying a place like a parliament, nor of the episcopal conference being given jurisdiction and teaching authority in its own right. Such authority can only come from Christ, and though history and present Church practice demonstrate that episcopal conferences can teach collegially, they cannot bind the conscience in a formal way unless they meet the essential conditions cited above. *Apostolos Suos* summarizes:

> Taking into account that the authentic Magisterium of the bishops, namely what they teach insofar as they are invested with the authority of Christ, must always be in communion with the head of the college and its members, when the doctrinal declarations of episcopal conferences are approved unanimously they may certainly be issued in the name of the conferences themselves, and the faithful are obliged to adhere with a sense of religious respect to that au-

thentic Magisterium of their own bishops. However, if this unanimity is lacking, a majority alone of the bishops of a conference cannot issue a declaration as authentic teaching of the conference to which all the faithful of the territory would have to adhere, unless it obtains the *recognitio* of the Apostolic See, which will not give it if the majority requesting it is not substantial. The intervention of the Apostolic See is analogous to that required by law in order for the episcopal conference to issue general decrees.[217]

Priests: Participants in the Office of Ruling

No treatment of the office of the bishop as high priest, in the capacity of a shepherd in ruling and guiding, would be complete without a treatment of the priesthood. In the next paragraph, the Council treats of the priesthood in general, discussing the relation of priests to Christ, to bishops, to one another and to the faithful.

Priests are the prime collaborators in the office of shepherd with the bishop, and they are treated here as such. Deacons are treated after priests to preserve a natural progression, and to show how each order participates in the prime order of the bishop. "Thus the divinely instituted ecclesiastical ministry is exercised in different degrees by those who even from ancient times have been called priests, bishops and deacons."[218] Though the priest does not share in the fullness of the High Priesthood of Christ, as the bishop does, still each priest is "consecrated"[219] by the sacrament of Orders for the ministry of Word and Sacrament. "Bishops are superior to priests by divine institution both regarding order and jurisdiction."[220]

Lumen Gentium clearly teaches that bishops, priests and deacons all have a special relationship to Christ. Regarding the bishop and the priest, this entails the power "to preach the Gospel and shepherd the faithful as well as celebrate divine worship as true priests of the New Testament."[221] Since Vatican II, the precise relationship of the priest to Christ has been greatly questioned. Many think that the priest is just a community leader with no special power. It is not uncommon to find new theories of the Eucharist which claim that the community is the gathered assembly and the priest, as their representative, consecrates the Eucharist in their name. They give him the power. Sermons abound that claim that the assembly is the body of Christ and the only reason the tabernacle exists in a church is for Communion for the sick. Others believe that Vatican II supported the idea of a temporary priesthood and bypass the whole notion of a special relationship to Christ for a new, more advanced democratic idea of the priest as assembly president. In fact, many Catholics now embrace a Protestant idea that there is no such thing as an official Christian priesthood.

The Council Fathers taught in paragraph 10 that the difference between the universal priesthood of believers and the ministerial priesthood was a difference not simply of degree, but also one of nature.[222] Now, they expand this concept to treat of what that essential difference might mean. *Lumen Gentium* paragraph 28 states that priests act "in the person of Christ" and "make present again and apply [...] the unique sacrifice of the New Testament."[223] This action in the person of Christ is the necessary basis for their hierarchical ministry.

Contemporary Catholicism is very wary of being too specific about the nature of the priesthood. This affects not only the life of priests already ordained, but also seminary education. If one has no clear idea of what one is producing, it is difficult to know what process to use to shape the product.

In a prescient article he wrote in 1985, "What Is a Priest? An Urgent Effort at Clarification,"[224] Josef Pieper described a situation very much like the one priests are facing today. He compares the present malaise in priestly identity to the problem one would have in pinpointing what makes a physician. The identifying quality cannot be simply the individual who practices the art of healing, because even parents do that within families. Though mere description is important, this assumption does not arrive at a defining condition that sets the physician off from others. Rather, this condition is a right, given from outside: "[H]e alone possesses, for example, the right to cut into another person's abdomen (which, if anyone else did it, would be a physical assault); the right to prescribe drugs, even drugs which might contain toxic substances; the right to determine if someone is dead, and so on."[225]

In the same way, the Catholic tradition is very clear about the specific difference that sets the priesthood apart from other vocations. "No one can consecrate this sacrament [the Eucharist] except a priest who is rightly ordained according the keys of the Church which Jesus Christ himself gave to the apostles and their successors."[226]

Some acts are immediately ordered to God in two
ways. In one way on behalf of only one person, like
to compose individual prayers, to vow and other like
things. Each of the baptized is capable of performing such an act. In another way, on the behalf of the
whole Church, and thus the priest alone possesses
acts immediately ordered to God, because he alone
is able to bring about an act of the whole Church
who consecrates the Eucharist which is a sacrament
of the whole Church.[227]

Along a similar line, Pius XII in the encyclical *Mediator Dei*
said in answer to a teaching in his time that the priest only acts as a
representative of the community, "But we think it necessary to repeat
that the priest only acts for the people because he bears the person
of Jesus Christ, who is head of all his members and offers himself
in their stead."[228]

Vatican II teaches, in union with this constant tradition, that
priests have a special conformity to Christ like no other member of
the Mystical Body because through a special character they are able
to act in the person of Christ for the whole Church. "Through that
sacrament [Holy Orders] priests by the anointing of the Holy Spirit
are signed with a special character and so are configured to Christ the
priest in such a way that they are able to act in the person of Christ
the head."[229] This special relation of the priest to Christ demands that
Holy Orders involve more than just a juridical state, but a true state of
consecration, a true ontological change. In the ordination of a priest,
the priest is consecrated in a special way which conforms him in a
deeper way to Christ than a layman.

In both the rite of ordination and the nature of the change entailed
in the priesthood, the new life of the priest is based on a two-fold act:
dedication (*dedicatio*) and consecration (*consecratio*).[230] Consecration presupposes dedication, which is "an act of self-surrender on
the part of the man to be ordained."[231] In this act, the person himself
withdraws himself by his own free will from the act of customary
usage in everyday life and his very self "can no longer be put to the
personal use for which it was formerly employed."[232] God, by the
ministry of the bishop, takes this act of self-surrender, accepts it and
through the rite of ordination, the "consecrated person receives a new
attribute which alters his nature."[233]

By this change, the priest enters a special consecrated state in which he serves the communion of the Church in a new and unique way. This does not deny the manner is which he serves with everyone else as a member of the holy People of God through Baptism. Many Church documents are fond of quoting a statement of St. Augustine's about being bishop: "I am in fear because I am for you. I am consoled to be with you. Because for you I am a bishop, with you I am a Christian. The first name is one of responsibility, the second, one of grace. The former is the name of a danger, the latter of salvation."[234] Rather, the new and special title of the ministerial priesthood presupposes and deepens the consecration of Baptism because it entails a true sacred power (*sacra potestas*)[235] independent of personal worthiness based on the character of Orders. This character is of the nature of a tool, but one given only for the service intended which is primarily and immediately to consecrate the Eucharist.

In the consecration of the Eucharist, this sacred power is seen in its fullness because such a miracle can only be accomplished by someone acting *in persona Christi capitis* (in the person of Christ the Head of the Church). "In the person of Christ he [the ministerial priest] effects the Eucharistic sacrifice and offers it to God in the name of all the people."[236]

Pieper thinks in his article that the concept of acting in the place of another is foreign to us today. Even in modern drama there is a new non-Aristotelian theory of acting whereby the actor should never leave the secular world which is real and everyday. He should merely speak his lines as though quoting someone else and never seek to identify himself with the character. In the traditional theory of acting, the actor speaks the lines while psychologically viewing himself in the role as though he were someone else.

Much of the modern theory of the priesthood looks on the priest's identification with Christ in a similar way. Such theories argue that the people consecrate the Eucharist, which is only a meal; the priest is merely their president or representative, with no special ontological powers; the priesthood of the laity and of the ministers differ only by degree, and not by essence; priesthood may even be viewed as a temporary vocation, because it involves no indelible mark or character in the one ordained and, thus, no special life style of life or dress; the unifying factor in the Eucharist is the personal charisma of the priest;

and since there is no special power or metaphysical identification with Christ as male involved by acting in the person of Christ, the priesthood should be open to the psychological charisma of women.

The true Catholic understanding is that the priest is a man, set apart for sacred service not only in his own psychology, but also ontologically. This demands a deeper conversion of life and also necessitates that the priest completely surrender acting in his own person when he celebrates the Eucharist. As Christ did not come to be served, but to serve, identification with him means that priesthood is not an honor, but a service. This service is primarily seen in the surrender of self in the celebration of Mass. The beauty of the liturgy is that the self is transcended not only in a psychological way, but even in an ontological way. In fact, the psychological transcendence is based on the ontological, since action follows being. This identification cannot be sensed, but demands faith. Nonetheless, it is a real identification in being. The priest is the servant of communion with the higher Persons of the Trinity, at the basis of the union of the social communion of the assembly. Neither the assembly nor the priest creates or sustains this. Christ does.

The relation of the priest to the Eucharist is essential because it is the culmination and font (*culmens et fons*) of Catholic life.[237] In all the other sacraments the priest speaks in the person of the minister (*ex persona ministri*), but in the Eucharist he merely repeats the words of institution. In Baptism, the priest says, "I baptize you," in Penance, "I absolve you," etc. But in the Eucharist, the priest must transcend his "I."

> [...] in the other sacraments the consecration of the matter consists only in a blessing, from which the matter consecrated derives instrumentally a spiritual power, which through the priest who is an animated instrument, can pass on to inanimate instruments. But in this sacrament the consecration of the matter consists in the miraculous change of the substance, which can only be done by God; hence the minister in performing this sacrament has no other act save the pronouncing of the words. [...] The form of the sacrament is pronounced as if Christ were speaking in person, so that it is given to be understood that

the minister is doing nothing in perfecting this sacrament, except to pronounce the words of Christ.[238]

Of course, this identification in being with Christ caused by the
character of Holy Orders is something only open to the knowledge
of faith. However, in the sacrament, this metaphysical aspect of faith
must be expressed in the stylized ritual gestures of the Mass. For example, though the vestments are articles of clothing which date from
a certain historical period in history, their use at the Mass takes on the
aspect of expressing the transcendent nature of the action performed
by the human, ministerial priest. He is not acting during the sacrifice
as the individual whose name is found on his passport, but *in persona
Christi*. This is why it is much more than a violation of the canons of
etiquette for the priest to *ad lib* at Mass. The "Hi, how are you this
morning? Isn't it a beautiful day?" are greetings the priest would use
acting in his own person. At Mass, he is acting in the person of the
transcendent Christ, the high priest, and it is a greater violation of
this action for the priest to greet someone in his own person than for
someone playing Hamlet to interrupt the play to say, "Hi, how are you?
Isn't it a nice day?" The action in the person of Christ provides the
specific difference to the action of Holy Orders. Laymen may quote
the words of institution of the Eucharist or wear the vestments, but
they do not have the character and so there is no ontological identification with Christ and thus no change or sacrifice.

Of course, if one does not believe in transubstantiation, an ontological and miraculous change of the bread into the Body of Christ,
or that the Mass is a sacrifice, then no special character is necessary.
Yet, both Vatican II and the tradition of the Church clearly teach the
ontological difference between the ministerial and lay priesthood.
The primary purpose of the existence of this priesthood is to celebrate
the Eucharist. "Priests are ordained to confect the sacrament of the
Body of Christ."[239]

Two points must also be clarified here. It is often said that according to Vatican II, preaching is the prime duty of the priest and,
a fortiori, of the bishop. At the same time a custom has arisen of
allowing persons who are not ordained to give sermons at the time
of the homily during Mass, as though this were a speech like any
other. The principle of the priest as actor in the person of Christ also
applies here.

It is true that Vatican II says, "For since nobody can be saved who has not first believed, it is the first task of priests as co-workers of the bishops to preach the Gospel of God to all men."[240] This "first" must not be understood in any other sense except as priority of time. One must first believe before one performs the actions the Gospel demands, especially the sacraments. Thus preaching is a first step in conversion of the members of the Church. However, what is prior in time is not what is prior in being. In priority of time, the grain comes before the ear; in priority of being (metaphysical priority) the ear comes before the grain. In the metaphysical sense the prime action of the priest is the celebration of Mass. "However, it is in the eucharistic cult or in the eucharistic assembly of the faithful (*synaxis*) that they exercise in the supreme (*maxime*) their sacred functions."[241] The celebration of the Eucharist is thus prior in the metaphysical sense, for the priestly character is seen there above all.

This truth also contains the solution to the relation of preaching to the celebration of Mass and the reason preaching at Mass is reserved to the priest or deacon, i.e. those who possess the character of Orders. Priests and deacons have the right to preach everywhere, and because preaching at Mass is integrally connected to the reading of the Word which forms the proper context for the action of the sacrament celebrated in the person of Christ, only he who has the character of conformity to the person of Christ can preach in this context. "The Eucharist appears as the summit of all preaching of the Gospel."[242] This particular form of preaching can only be done by one who possesses the character. Others may preach in other contexts, but not this one.

To distinguish between "homily" and "reflection" in this matter is only a matter of words, and to allow the non-ordained to "reflect" during the normal time of the homily merely confuses the issue. One canonist interprets the present norm in the Code in this way:

> This (Canon 767, n. 1) is constitutive law, defining the three constitutive elements of a homily. A homily is: (1) that form of preaching (2) which is part of the liturgy itself and (3) is reserved to a priest or deacon. Thus, a homily is only one form of preaching, namely, preaching at liturgy by a cleric. Preaching outside liturgy cannot be called a homily, nor can

preaching during the liturgy by a layperson be called
a homily, but must be called a reflection, an instruction, an exhortation, or the like. The diocesan bishop
may not dispense from this norm, evidently because
it is constitutive law.[243]

Both Church law and the intelligent evaluation of the teaching of
the Church about the unity of word and sacrament underline the fact
that it is not consonant with the will of Christ for those not ordained
to preach a homily during Mass or give a speech during the time of the
homily. Though someone not ordained may legitimately give a report,
or speak about things of parish concern during Mass, this should not
be done at the time of the homily lest there be confusion.

Since the Eucharist is the body of Christ, and preaching at Mass
is intimately united with Christ and his body the Church, priests must
submit to the bishop in both the manner in which Mass is celebrated
in a Church under his care, and to the Church in general in the person
of the bishop in the content of the sermon. The homily must express
authentic Catholic doctrine and not merely reflect the private opinion
of the priest. "No one, not even a Priest, may on his own authority add,
omit, or change anything in the liturgy."[244] At present, some priests
will arbitrarily alter elements in the liturgy imagining they can add or
subtract on their own authority from the order of service, and do this
for either a liberal or traditionalist intent. In either case, the principle
is clear that the Church as a whole has complete authority over the
prayer life of the Church. The *munus* of ruling (*presbyter*) is joined to
the *munus* of sanctifying (*sacerdos*).[245] Preaching and teaching relate
to both these powers because the same faith underlies each.

The attitude of some clelebrants which underlies creative order
of service, is also expressed in creative teaching of doctrine. The
faithful have a right to the truth and priests express true communion
of life *in* the Church when they have communion of practice *with*
the Church, as a whole, and acknowledge the authority of the bishop
or the Holy See both in carrying out liturgical ritual and in teaching
from the pulpit.

The nature of the character of the sacrament of Orders is the
source of the communion between the bishop and the priest. The
bishop has the fullness of the character. Priests in the New Testament
are always in plural number and gather around one altar with one

bishop.[246] The bishop is the head of the college of his priests. "The priests, prudent cooperators of the episcopal college and its support and mouthpiece, [...] constitute, together with the bishop, a unique sacerdotal college (*presbyterium*) dedicated it is true to a variety of distinct duties."[247] Ignatius of Antioch says that the priests with the bishop form a "Senate of God and Council of the Apostles."[248]

In the local church this variety of duties of the *presbyterium* means that priests carry out their pastoral office "under the authority of the Bishop and not in their own names."[249] There is then a difference in function caused by the different participation in the character of Holy Orders. On the part of the priest, the duty involves "obedience and trust."[250] This is a response to the bishops having "paternal and friendly affection"[251] for his priests.

Religious obedience demands that the subject see in the acts of the superior a moral secondary cause whereby God carries out his governing of the world. Just as God does not directly act in nature, for example, causing "heat" to be hot (but uses fire for that purpose), so in the moral realm, God acts through secondary agents. This is not a defect of divine power, but the result of God's strength.

> God is the sovereign master of his plan. But to carry it out he also makes use of his creatures' cooperation. This use is not a sign of weakness, but rather a token of almighty God's greatness and goodness. For God grants his creatures not only their existence, but also the dignity of acting on their own, of being causes and principles for each other and thus of cooperating in the accomplishment of his plan.[252]

A good example of this comes from the old admonition before marriage, which reminds the couple that through their sacrament God allows them to participate in and continue the work of creation. In the same way, all human superiors participate in God's providence, but this is especially true of bishops as Christ's representatives.

On the part of the hierarchy, these truths have several important practical implications. Some bishops attempting to avoid excessive authority today advocate "group government," or what one psychiatrist has called "fraternal authority."[253] This manner of exercising authority shifts all the responsibility for obedience to the subject. The subject should have as much freedom as possible, an ideal state if the subjects are all mature and responsible adults. Unfortunately, this mode of exercising authority frequently degenerates into an abdication of responsibility on the part of the very one charged with the good of all. It is true that a superior needs to engage the intelligence of the subject, as the will must be moved by the intellect, but this engagement also involves guidance and direction when this is necessary for the good of all.

Practical requirements that reflect the desire of the Council for "paternal and friendly affection" could be listed as the following.[254] Chief among these is benevolent love. Benevolence is necessary for a person to show friendly affection. This means that the authority must always consider the true good of those in his care. This benevolence demands correction when needed, as well as the authority's not absenting himself from the outcome if the subject is accused of wrongdoing. The present trend among some in the hierarchy to abandon their priests to the civil order for some civil crimes, merely on the pretext of accusation, flies in the face of this good will.

Coupled with this good will, the authority must show respect for the subject; priests are not just useful tools for bishops. They cannot be sacrificed to arbitrary goals like avoiding bad press or loss of revenue for the diocese. Whatever is asked of the subject should be explained, and if it is a command of extreme difficulty or regards some very important matter, this should not be left to subordinates. Priests should be able to approach their bishops for adequate explanations of decisions affecting them, and explanations should not be left merely to chancery officials. The first, friendly affection of the bishop should be for his priests. When bishops are too busy resolving political, domestic or financial issues to have time for legitimate crucial problems with their clergy, the relationship of communion in God established by the character is unfulfilled.

Thus, the authority should avoid foolish or excessive commands. In the practice of the liturgy, for example, when the ritual is sufficiently set out in the common liturgical books issued from the Holy See, the bishop should avoid burdening his clergy with many additional diocesan norms, which merely multiply the problems in the order of service. This might include a demand that everyone in the church stand until Communion has been distributed. Constant meddling in the priest's ability to administer his parish or, on the other hand, failing to correct liturgical abuses, merely demonstrate that a bishop distrusts the initiative, intelligence or good faith of his clergy. St. Thomas warns, "If a superior makes a heap of precepts and lays them on his subjects so that they are unable to fulfill them, they are excused from sin. Therefore superiors should refrain from making a multitude of precepts."[255]

The attitude of fraternal affection requires that the bishop exercise great prudence and discretion in giving commands. No one priest has the same personality as another. The obedience demanded of a choleric personality is the same obedience demanded of a sanguine personality. But in demanding this obedience, the superior should take into account the personality he is dealing with before issuing the order. A choleric personality who has a forceful disposition requires a different approach than that of a melancholic person who has an emotional and sympathetic temperament, or a sanguine who is superficial, or a phlegmatic who is shy and retiring. Priests surrender much when they embrace a way of life that places them under the command of another for the whole of their lives. The bishop should respect the depth and difficulty of the sacrifice and the good faith of the one who makes it.

By the same token, the priest has serious responsibilities toward his bishop. *Lumen Gentium* describes these under the rubric of "obedience and trust." The following are some characteristics of this obedience.

The priest must be open and receptive to the initiatives and commands of his bishop. He must be able not only to understand the meaning of the command, but have even an emotional acceptance of the fact that the authority represents a good for him because the authority represents the whole Church.

This openness must be based on the priest's trust that the bishop is not only interested in him, but also in the good of the whole Church whom the bishop represents. No one can easily obey if he does not perceive that the authority will protect him insofar as it is able. Of course, if the one in authority has demonstrated a constant predilection for only a certain group of priests, or a certain point of view, or again looks on himself more as a servant of the civil order or bureaucracy than the father of a family, this erodes trust in the subject.

For many today, the whole concept of obedience is repugnant. Thus, some priests act independently of the Church in the practice of the liturgy or the teaching of doctrine. Each subject must realize his own limitations, for excessively selfish and egocentric priests cannot obey because their intelligence cannot penetrate their emotional desires. Such individuals want to be the measure of the world, when only God can give that measure. Priests who continually act on their own feed only their own egos, not the common good. This includes egocentric actions in relation to the commands of the Holy See, as the Pope is the bishop of bishops.

This egoism is especially sad when exhibited by a lower superior regarding the authority of a higher superior—for example, if a religious superior orders a non-ordained person to preach at Mass under the vow of obedience. Here the superior suggests that his authority is more important than the authority of the Pope. History is replete with sad examples of superiors who have sacrificed their own authority by compromising the higher superior, simply because it is precisely the higher superior who guarantess the ability of the lower to command.

Any true obedience requires that a person realize his relative place in the order of things. In today's society of throw-away people (and wholesale abortion and contraception) it is very difficult for the individual to feel that he has self-worth or that his existence is good because he comes from the hands of a loving Creator. Many people compensate a sense of inferiority by demanding a place in the order of things that puts them on the same level as everyone else with the result that no one has to obey anyone else. Healthy self-respect, on the other hand, entails an honest evaluation of a person's capabilities and the fact that we all need to depend on others to exist, to live, to work and to grow. This is certainly true in civil society. Man is by nature a political and social animal.

This sense of dependence is true not only in ordinary human things, but even more in the community of the Church. The whole tone of the teaching of Vatican II was a demand to view the Church as a supernatural society, supernatural in origin and supernatural in goal. No one can claim absolute independence regarding the realm of the Trinity; life in the Trinity can never be ours to do with as we please.

These attitudes should underpin a healthy respect for the necessity of authority. A priest needs to be able to understand that when he obeys and respects his bishop, he is obeying and respecting the whole Church. This is, *a fortiori*, more true of his need to respect and obey the Pope whose office as a bishop is to command the whole Church. The priest is thus connecting himself with something much higher, deeper and more all-encompassing than himself. Ultimately, he is connecting himself to Christ who obeyed human superiors, even defective ones, because in their office they represented the authority of his Father. Of course, again this requires that bishops act like bishops in their very masculine role to defend the truth and virtue of the members of their diocese. This is done by correct teaching of dogma and morals, and implementing thoughtful discipline in the liturgy and the lives of their subjects.

If the character of Orders provides a marvelous foundation of the relation in "fraternal affection" of the bishop for his priests, this must also be true of the priests themselves. This dependence on the Church is manifested in a clear way by the dependence of priests on one another. No one understands a priest's trials and joys in his vocation like another priest. Priestly associations, both formal and informal, should be sought and encouraged.

> In virtue of their sacred ordination and of their common mission all priests are united together by bonds of intimate brotherhood, which manifests itself in a spontaneously and gladly given mutual help, whether spiritual or temporal, whether pastoral or personal, through the medium of reunions and community life, work and fraternal charity.[256]

Finally, priests also have a unique relationship, based on all these others, with the faithful. The priest exists to serve the faithful, not the faithful the priest. This ministry of service is especially seen in the Mass and the sacraments. Proclamation and preaching of doctrine that conforms to the teaching of the whole Church, especially the teaching of the Pope, flow from and support this relationship. The same is true of ready availability of the sacraments. Ordinarily, the priest cannot sacrifice the availability of Mass or Penance to his own needs for rest and relaxation. In fact, no matter what the personal opinions of a priest are on a given matter, he has a duty to teach the faithful what the Church as a whole believes. He is a specially deputed agent by which the "Light of the Nations" permeates the hearts of the faithful.

Deacons: Cooperators in the Priesthood

No treatment of Orders would be complete without some treatment of the restored diaconate. One of the great innovations of *Lumen Gentium* was the restoration of the order of deacon from merely a proximate preparation for the priesthood, which it retains, to a permanent stable group of men who will never be priests, participating in the character of the sacrament of Orders. With a view to the process of restoration, the Council first treated of the nature of the diaconate.

Like episcopal or priestly orders, the diaconate also communicates a character by which the recipient further is conformed to Christ as priest, prophet and king. The Council is clear that deacons do, indeed, share in the sacrament of Holy Orders. They are, however, "not ordained to the priesthood but to ministry."[257] Deacons are ordained to the "ministry of the bishops."[258] They are, thus, an important part of the offices of ministry serving the communion of the Church.

Vatican II restored the office of deacon to a permanent ministry in the Church and not merely a transitional step on the way to the priesthood. In the post-Vatican II Church the office of deacon has become an important part of the Church's sacramental life, fulfilling the vision of the Council Fathers who thought restoration of this office would be helpful in mission countries, like Latin America, where there were so many Catholics and so few priests. They left it to the Pope to determine whether married men could embrace this ministry and, in fact, the Pontiff has permitted them to do so.

Deacons are not to be just pious laymen or watered-down priests. They have a distinct proper contribution to make to the apostolate. This includes "the service of the liturgy, of the word and of charity."[259]

The service of the liturgy is carried out in the solemn administration of Baptism, the distribution of Holy Communion and preaching. Deacons can also preside over marriages, assist at funerals and dispense numerous sacramentals. The restored diaconate is to aid the care of souls wherever the Church suffers a shortage of priests. In the solemn administration of Baptism and distribution of the Holy Eucharist, the deacon shows the priestly character of the Christ he serves. In preaching he carries out the office of prophet, and in the administration of charity—by witnessing marriages, assisting at funerals, and offering other services—he manifests the kingly character of service for the common good.

CHAPTER FIVE
The Mystical Body of Christ II

The Laity

The first great division of the document on the Church in Vatican II treats of the being of the Church. That being includes the individuals for whom the hierarchy exists: the laity. Everyone in the hierarchy is ordained to a ministry of service, a service that includes all the members of the Church and therefore includes the laity.

The first task is to try to make an adequate definition of the laity. This problem is challenging today especially because two basic difficulties plague the modern Church. The first is a denial of any distinction between the priesthood of the laity and the ministerial priesthood. For instance, one new liturgical theory teaches that the community consecrates the Eucharist, the priest serving as merely the people's representative. This doctrinal error has already been dealt with. The priestly character is a deeper participation in the baptismal character and entails in it the ability to consecrate the Eucharist in the person of Christ the High Priest.

A second difficulty has to do with the exact place of religious life in the Church. Those who profess the evangelical counsels come from both the clergy and the laity. Thus, priests profess these counsels as do some who are not ordained. This has led some to opine that there is no special consecration proper to religious life. This would mean that special clothes, like habits, are superfluous and perhaps even mistaken. Life in convents or monasteries would seem to be counter-indicated also, as this suggests some special consecration for religious not enjoyed by the laity as a whole. Later the present text will make clear that though religious have a special consecration, this is not in relation to the being of the Church, but to its act.

Vatican II thus defines the laity as those who share the consecration of the character of Baptism, but have not implemented it by deepening the character or by living it in a special unusual way. "The term 'laity' is here understood to mean all the faithful except those in Holy Orders and those who belong to a religious state approved by the Church."[260]

Vatican II was very clear that the laity constitute a true state of life in the Church, as their consecration is more general and oriented to the secular world. However, this recognition of a lay state is to be understood as referring to state in the broad sense of the term. "'The state of the laity is used in place of condition and mission (terms which occur a little further on) so that the honor of constituting a state is recognized for the laity at least in the broad sense."[261]

The Council wanted to make clear that all are called to participate in holiness, but each according to a specific charism. The Council quotes Ephesians 4: 15-16: "Practice the truth in love, and so grow up in all things in him who is the head, Christ. For from him the whole body—being closely joined and knit together through every joint of the system according to the functioning in due measure of each single part—derives its increase to the building up of itself in love." Pope John XXIII said that this text was "programmatic"[262] and should be "written above the doors of the Council."[263]

Lumen Gentium's definition of the laity looks at the lay faithful primarily as distinct from the rest of the Church, but Fr. Jordan Aumann has developed a more positive definition of the laity, one which seeks not just to set the laity off in relief from those with a special consecrated role in the Church, but also to identify their consecration.

> To summarize: the laity, like all the other members of Christ's faithful, are baptized persons (sacramental aspect) who are thereby incorporated into Christ (Christian aspect) and made members of the Church (ecclesiological aspect) with the right and duty to participate actively in the mission of the Church (missionary aspect). But in addition to all that, the laity, by reason of their secular characteristic, are committed to the renewal and sanctification of the temporal order.[264]

There are two important consequences of both definitions. The first is that the laity have a place in the Church which is characterized as "mission." They are distinguished from both the clergy and religious because their true consecration in the Church is of a "secular nature."[265] The "world" here is taken not only to mean the world as a kingdom ruled by sin, but also in a more positive sense, everyday life. The laity are called and gifted to sanctify the world from within.

A second consequence follows from this. The sacred ministry of the sacraments and the separation from secular occupations and interests are part of the nature and mission of the clergy and religious. As the laity are to sanctify the world from within, it would be equally a mistake for clergy to become "hyphenated priests"[266] occupied mostly in secular pursuits, or for lay people to be clericalized so they take over all functions in the liturgy and the parish except actual consecration of the Eucharist. Some have suggested that priests or religious should not teach Sacred Theology in Catholic institutions, but should leave this to the laity. Edward Schillebeeckx, O.P. discussed the dangers of the clericalization of the laity in an article he wrote on the laity in 1965:

> It has not yet been understood with sufficient depth
> that, precisely because he is a non-clerical member
> of the People of God, the layman has a constitutive
> relationship with the secular world, which perme-
> ates also his participation in the Church's primary
> mission. The result is that the layman's specific
> contribution to the work of spreading the Gospel is
> undervalued and, when he is genuinely active, he
> adopts clerical ways which prejudice his character
> as an authentic layman.[267]

Though the Church has encouraged the laity to enter formally into the ritual of the Mass by acting as lectors and extraordinary ministers of the Eucharist, lay persons exercise their proper and characteristic dignity in transforming the secular world of the family and the professions, where they find their proper place. The laity live in the world and work in it; they sanctify the world against the evils which are present in it. In this they imitate Christ who had to act among ordinary people in an ordinary life in order to save us. "It was in keeping with the end of the Incarnation that Christ should not lead a solitary life, but should associate with men. Now it is most fitting that he who associates with others should conform to their manner of living."[268]

The laity are not, therefore, some stand-alone vocation in the Church. They are truly called to sanctity, along with priests and religious albeit in different ways. They truly serve with the bishops and priests as "brothers."[269] The laity exercise the true priesthood of the faithful, and one of the principal places where they sanctify one another and the Church is in marriage. The ministers of marriage are the couple, and baptized spouses are each the minister of sanctification for the other. Together they form a "domestic church" with their children. They are the first apostles of their children and accordingly have a right and duty to teach them the faith.

The religious actions which the laity do in the Church are normal and necessary. They are the regular orderly way in which the society of the Church carries on the saving of the world. Their participation in the apostolate is due to the character of Baptism and Confirmation. This foundation is completed and nourished in the Eucharist. Since the Holy Spirit is the soul of the apostolate, the laity are moved by the Holy Spirit to carry out the saving work of Christ. They are in every true sense of the world the salt of the earth as they make the Church present everywhere by "personal contacts."[270]

There are some who would like to make the religious mission of the laity "occasional and supplemental."[271] For example, some chancery offices or officials feel the laity need some special mandate from the hierarchy to prepare their own children for the sacraments. Though priests and catechists with a special mandate from the Church have a right to examine those who present themselves for the sacraments, the right of the laity to teach their children is founded on both the natural and divine law. They need no special mandate for this. However, a ministry which is an extension of the bishop's mandate to teach, for example, in a Catholic school or religion program, would need a special mandate as this is public evangelization and an apostolate in a stricter sense.

> The Subcomission distinguished clearly enough between a general apostolate and apostolate in the stricter sense, namely from a mandate. The common vocation therefore is distinguished from special forms which are under the 'more immediate' responsibility of the hierarchy.[272]

The laity, then, are not to wait for the initiative of the hierarchy, but spontaneously to undertake their mission in those areas that are proper to them. They can also cooperate more closely in the mission of the hierarchy, if they are called to do so by the hierarchy, for "they have, moreover, the capacity of being appointed to some ecclesiastical offices with a view to a spiritual end."[273]

> This mission includes the three-fold nature of the mission of Christ: priest, prophet and king. The Subcomission at Vatican II was clear that this mission should not involve a "too rigid application of this three-fold mission, lest a tripartite theology be applied."[274] Rather, the use of the terms means more generally worship (priest), witness (prophet) and service (king).[275]

The priestly aspect of the laity is seen not in offering the sacrifice of the Mass by changing the bread and wine into the body and blood of Christ. Laity are not in themselves ministers of the altar. Instead, it is seen in all the actions of their everyday life when viewed from God's point of view. These actions are most fittingly offered[276] with the Victim in the sacrifice of the Mass. "And so, worshipping everywhere by their holy actions, the laity consecrate the world itself to God."[277] The consecration of the world through the actions of the laity is not due to the actions themselves, but to the attitude of the one who does them. This attitude is looking at the world from God's point of view, under the aspect of eternity.

This theology of Vatican II is not new; it reflects centuries of normal development of spiritual doctrine on the part of the masters.

> God still speaks as he spoke to our Fathers, when there were neither spiritual directors nor set methods. Then they saw that each moment brings with it a duty to be faithfully fulfilled. That was enough for spiritual direction. On that duty their whole attention was fixed at each successive moment like the hand of a clock which marks the hours. Under the continuous impulse of God, their spirit found itself turning to each new object as it was presented to them by God at each hour of the day.[278]

The prophetic aspect of the mission of the laity includes their witness to the last things. Until the end of time, God fulfills the prophetic aspect of Christ's mission not only in the formal teaching of the hierarchy, but also in the witness of the laity who teach the faith. Central to this prophetic minstry is the instruction in the faith which parents should give their children.

> For the husband is the head of the wife as Christ is the head of the Church. Husbands, love your wives as Christ loved the Church and gave himself up for her, that he might sanctify her, having cleansed her by the washing of water with the word, that he might present the Church to himself in splendor, without spot or wrinkle or any such thing, that she might be holy and without blemish. Even so husbands should love their wives as their own bodies. For no man ever hates his own flesh, but nourishes and cherishes it, as Christ does the Church, because we are members of his body. For this reason a man shall leave his father and mother and be joined to his wife, and the two shall become one. This is a great mystery, and I mean in reference to Christ and the Church. (Ephesians 5:23-32)

If one journeys to the Church of the Holy Sepulcher in Jerusalem, one can find there the site of the crucifixion, the rock of Golgotha. There are holes in the rock. If one listens, one can hear the sound of rushing water underneath the rock. The early Christians believed that the site of the tree of the crucifixion was the same place where the tree of temptation had stood in the Garden of Eden and they also theologically taught that the water under the rock was the origin of all the rivers of the world. When the Heart of Christ, filled with redemptive love and grace for mankind, was pierced with a lance, they believed that the water and blood flowed down the side of the cross, through the holes in the rock, and entered the waters of the world. This mixture of water and blood gave the rivers a mysterious power to actually to accomplish the sanctification in grace of those whom it touched in Baptism.

The Church and the sacraments were born from the wounded side of the dead Christ, much as Eve was born from the side of the sleeping

Adam in Genesis. St. Paul speaks about this birth in the Letter to the
Ephesians where he compares the Church to marriage. "Christ gave
himself up for her (the Church) that he might cleanse and sanctify
her by the washing of water with the Word." Marriage is a *magnum
sacramentum*, a great sign of the mystery of the Cross. Thomas
Aquinas says, "Here it must be noted that four sacraments are said
to be great: namely Baptism by reason of effect, because it destroys
fault and opens the gate of Paradise; Confirmation, by reason of the
minister, because it can only be conferred by bishops and no one else;
the Eucharist, by reason of what it contains, because it contains the
whole Christ; and Matrimony, by reason of what it signifies, because
it is a sign of the union of Christ and the Church."[279]

Marriage is not only a sign of Christ and his Church in the New
Testament, but a primordial sign of the union within the Trinity of
the Father, the Son and the Holy Spirit expressed incompletely, but
implicitly in the Old Testament. In Genesis, God says, "It is not good
for man to be alone." (Gn. 2:18) Why not? Because man is made in
the image and likeness of God, and God is a Trinity of persons. If
man cannot experience communion of persons, then he cannot truly
realize the fact that he is in the image and likeness of God, himself a
communion of Persons. In Genesis 2, God brings all the animals to
man to be named because these are all the creatures which possess a
body like man. But Adam finds none like himself. God therefore casts
Adam into a deep sleep and takes part of his flesh to make Eve. The
two become one and for the first time can experience true communion
of spiritual life in beings who have bodies. When Adam sees Eve, he
utters the first great cry of joy. "This at last is bone of my bone, and
flesh of my flesh." (Gn. 2:23)

They recognize each other as similar and yet different, so they
can experience interpersonal communion as creatures with bodies,
but which are called to spiritual union. Thus, the first proclamation
of marriage as an indissoluble union is made. "Therefore a man
leaves his father and his mother and cleaves to his wife, and they
become one flesh." (Gn. 2:24) Since the Father, the Son and the Holy
Spirit enjoy an interpersonal communion in which they never leave
one another, marriage must image this to be complete. This means
that divorce is a natural evil. *The Catechism of the Catholic Church*
teaches: "Divorce is a grave offense against the natural law. It claims
to break the contract, to which the spouses freely consented, to live

with each other till death." (CCC #2384) The personal communion of the spouses, the unitive dimension of their bond, mirrors the Persons of the Trinity. Before the sin, Adam and Eve enjoyed this personal intimacy without fear of manipulation or the will to dominate through power. They enjoyed this because they were filled with grace. Their marriage covenant was an expression of grace (the communion of hearts) and the principal means by which they lived grace. "The man and his wife were both naked and not ashamed." (Gn. 2:25) There was no sin, for they were created engraced. Nor could they use or abuse one another as long as they enjoyed this condition.

Imaging God demands not only indissolubility in marriage, but also imitating God in giving self. God does not keep his being, his truth or his goodness to himself, but is so good, that he constantly wants to share himself with other things. The principal motive in creation was that God should share himself with others and thus shows forth His goodness. Adam and Eve must also do this in their marriage if they are truly to image God. They do this by procreation, which demands sexual intercourse. In addition to union, then, marriage is only a complete image of God if oriented also to the creation of life as God is.

After the sin, Adam and Eve lose grace and so are "naked and ashamed." (Gn. 3:10) Domination through the sexual relationship enters the human race. Both the unitive and the procreative good are in jeopardy. The woman is told by God as a punishment for the sin, "Your desire shall be for your husband and he shall rule over you." (Gn. 3:16) Though grace is lost to the human race until the coming of Christ, and the original union of man and woman bears fruit only with great difficulty, because of the desire to manipulate and dominate which is part and parcel of lust (a fruit of the sin), marriage still remains in its original orientation. The Nuptial Blessing at the Wedding Mass clearly states this, "Father, by your plan man and woman are united, and married life established as the one blessing that was not forfeited by original sin or washed away in the flood." Marriage, a natural sacrament, waits for Christ to come and redeem it by bringing grace back to the human race. He does so on the cross.

Marriage is redeemed with all other natural things in man on the cross; it is redeemed also as an exercise of the priesthood of Christ. Just as the couple was a means of holiness to one another in the original creation, now their holiness is realized in and through Christ. Grace before the sin was something man experienced without pain. "They were naked and not ashamed." Now Christ holds the hands of the couple together with his, signed with the marks of his wounds. Human love, thus, is now taken up into Christ's sacrifice. The weakness of the Original Sin, called concupiscence, now demands that all growth in grace be a share in the cross, a struggle, a spiritual combat. This includes living a good marriage.

Since they are participating the passion of Christ in learning how to give and receive in a disinterested way again, and since they are growing in grace in learning this, married couples are true priests to one another. In the 19th century there was a long debate about what made marriage a holy estate. This was to meet the secularist challenge of the liberal state and the attempt on the part of the state to regulate marriage by civil marriage unions and divorce. Was it the Church which made marriage holy? Was it the priest who made marriage holy? Or must marriage even be celebrated in a church or before a priest if the state itself is holy, based on the baptismal character of the parties?

The Church reiterated a long-standing teaching that marriage is itself holy because the ministers are the baptized couple, made holy by Baptism. In Baptism, they not only receive grace, but also an interior conformity to Christ as priest, prophet and king, called the "character," or the indelible mark, which makes Baptism a sacrament which cannot be repeated. In the exchange of vows, couples are the means of holiness for each other, so they truly are the ministers. The priest and the Church must be present as witnesses because it would be unfitting for Christians to exchange vows of love in any other context than that of Christ and the Church. The union of the couple is not merely religious, but supernaturally holy, because of the character of Baptism present in the parties. Marriage is thus the prime exercise of the priesthood of the faithful, which was common to all the baptized.

The priestly character of marriage not only affects the unity of the spouses, but also relates directly to the procreative dimension. The purpose of procreation is not realized in just the existence of children, but also demands nurture and education. Since the body and the soul are the result of the marriage act, and the soul is created for union with God, St. Thomas does not hesitate to repeat with Aristotle that "there is something divine in human seed."[280] This divine character of human seed can only be finally completed in the Vision of God when man sees God face to face. Parents are the primary ministers who prepare their children for this mystery. Education does not end at Harvard or Yale, but in heaven. The child must be schooled for the *cultus Dei*, the worship of God. This schooling is an education in the virtues. This makes the home a domestic Church. Pope John Paul explains, "The Christian family constitutes a specific revelation and realization of ecclesial communion, and for that reason can and should be called a domestic church."(CCC #2204)[281]

We have said that parents are the first apostles of their children. As children grow in grace and are prepared for the worship of God in this life and the next, the couples themselves grow in grace. The education of children in the family, which includes moral leadership, is the primary means of the lay apostolate and the primary exercise of the priesthood of the faithful. "Parents have the first responsibility for the education of their children. They bear witness to this responsibility first by creating a home where tenderness, forgiveness, respect, fidelity, and disinterested service are the rule. The home is well suited for education in the virtues. This requires an apprenticeship in self-denial, sound judgment, and self-mastery—the precondition of true freedom. Parents should reach their children to subordinate the 'material and instinctual dimensions to interior and spiritual ones.'" (CCC #2223)

Pope John Paul II expresses it well.

> The sacrament of marriage gives to the educational role the dignity and vocation of being really and truly a "ministry" of the Church at the service of building up of her members. So great and splendid is the educational ministry of Christian parents that Saint Thomas has no hesitation in comparing it with the ministry of priests: "Some only propagate and guard spiritual life by a spiritual ministry: this is the role of the sacrament of Orders; others do this for both corporal and spiritual life, and this is brought about by the sacrament of marriage, by which a man and

a woman join in order to beget offspring and bring them up to worship God."[282]

The family has a primary role in education which is completed in heaven, and this role cannot be replaced by the State or any other human agency. This includes the right of the parents to choose a school for their children. This school must accord with the Christian mission in the case of sacramental marriage and accord with the natural law in the case of other marriages.

The priesthood of Christ entails the fact that Christ is both a priest and victim. The spouses cooperate in this mission of Christ by offering themselves for one another and for the good of their children. Though, of course, they are not ministerial priests, they still exercise a ministry through the ordinary virtues of their state which contribute to the formation of others in holiness.

> Among the virtues we should prefer that which suits our duty best, and not that which is most to our taste and although everyone ought to have all the virtues, yet not everyone is bound to practice them to the same extent. Each ought to give himself especially to the kind of life to which he is called.[283]

Many people are tempted to always go outside the family to find opportunities for Christian service. Many would like extraordinary phenomenon to accompany their Christian life. The family seems so dull and ordinary. Sports come before Mass. No one is ever home for a meal. Our very mobility has created a hunger for the always new and exciting, and spiritual boredom occurs when everything has been tried. No wonder people feel unloved and uncared for when the family is so dispersed. God rarely operates in the spectacular. Even the sacraments, from the point of view of the sign, seem very ordinary. Formation in the ordinary virtues is no ordinary thing, but part of the priesthood of the laity in pursuing holiness. One must remember that the prime virtue of the atonement was loving obedience expressed in humility. Happy family life based on these virtues is a very extraordinary thing, a work of art fashioned by grace. The priestly role of the laity in strengthening the communion of the society of the Church is seen in the foundation of the family.

As to the teaching charism, then, each vocation in the Church has a unique participation in this mission.

> There are many types of instruction. One is conversion to the faith, which Dionysius attributes to the bishop in Chapter II of *The Ecclesiastical Hierarchies*. This can befit any preacher or even any one of the faithful. The second is instruction by which someone is instructed in the rudiments of the faith and how to comport oneself in receiving the sacraments: this belongs secondarily to the ministers, primarily to the priests. The third is instruction in the mode of the Christian life and this belongs to the godparents. The fourth is the instruction in the profound mysteries of faith and on the perfection of Christian life. This belongs to bishops *ex officio*,—in virtue of their office.[284]

The kingly role is expressed in Christian service. One must realize that the power to rule is expressed first in ruling oneself and one's own inclinations to sin with the help of God's grace. "There are kings in whom sin does not reign, who rule their own body [...] These are kings and their king is God."[285] This is accomplished through the self-surrender to God brought about by the rule of the virtues and the gifts. The laity are called to bring forth the kingdom of Christ, first through the interior self-rule by which they can be a leaven in the secular professions. Though clerics and religious may sometimes be involved in secular pursuits, this is not their special place but only a supplementary role (*per modum suppletivum*).[286]

The kingly role of the laity then extends to preparing the secular professions as a climate in which the life of grace can be nourished through the practice of the virtues, especially the virtue of justice. Both societies, the Church and the State, are governed by different rights and laws, but there is a distinction between the two. "Because of the very economy of salvation the faithful should learn to distinguish carefully between the right and duties which they have as belonging to the Church and those which fall to them as members of the human society."[287] The distinction is based on the different purposes of these states or their final causes. Since all the other causes of a thing are determined by the final cause, the cause of these two societies also introduces different styles of authority which befit them, as well as different rights and duties. Another name for this final cause coupled with the order by which it is realized in society is the "common good." The orientation of man to this common good is part of his constitution as a reasoning being with a will guided by an intellect.

The Church has always maintained that man by *nature* is a part of two societies: the family and the State. Each has its origin and destiny in perfecting man in the natural order. In the case of the family, that origin is marriage, and the destiny is fidelity, fecundity and friendship. In the case of the State, it is the peace and tranquility of the citizens who harmoniously pursue their lives *in this world*. In contrast to the Social Contract theory, the Church has always maintained that man must be a part of both by very nature. One must remember that according to the Social Contract theory, man is not naturally a member of any society, but complete as an individual. He is forced by circumstances, either positive or negative, to form society to pursue greater goods or avoid greater evils. Society is always an external imposition on human freedom.

As the destinies of societies differ, so does their authority. In the family, the authority is determined by nature and resides in the parents. In the State, it is determined by constitution and may involve any type of government which pursues the common good and not the private good: monarchy, oligarchy, or democracy or some combination of these. As God is the author of nature, so God is the author of these societies, and the sanction on which their authority is based, albeit through natural reason.

> But God has likewise destined man for civil society according to the dictates of his very nature. In the plan of the Creator, society is a natural means which man can and must use to reach his destined end. Society is for man and not vice versa. This must not be understood in the sense of liberalistic individualism, which subordinates society to the selfish use of the individual; but only in the sense that by means of an organic union with society and by mutual collaboration the attainment of earthly happiness is placed within the reach of all.[288]

This pursuit of the common good which is in mankind by nature is called the social character. It is neither substantial to man in the sense that all of his actions are social or political, as totalitarians think, nor a simple accident or something incidental to man, as social contractualists and the liberal capitalists of the 19th century believed. It is a property, a *proprium* in the Scholastic sense, that is, the social character is not so identical with a being that man and society are the same thing substantially. But it is found always and everywhere the being is found. Wherever man is found, he must exist in society to pursue his perfection. Pope John Paul II calls this social character, "the attitude of solidarity."

> The attitude of solidarity is, so to speak, the natural consequence of the fact that human beings live and act together; it is the attitude of a community, in which the common good properly conditions and initiates participation and participation properly serves the common good, fosters it, and furthers its realization. Solidarity signifies the constant readiness to accept and to realize one's share in the community—what is one's share because of one's membership in a particular community.[289]

The common good, then, defines the community, and it is both the end and the order of the community. The end and the order complement each other. Both are necessary. The order serves the end and the end demands ordered community to be accomplished. It would be an error to oppose them to each other. Every end must: 1) be morally good; 2) be a true common good of human nature as a whole, and not just a sum of the good of private interest groups no matter how large; and 3) respect a proper relationship to other goods, for example, the good of the Church.

> Thus the priority of the common good, its superiority over the partial and individual goods does not result from the quantitative aspect of society; it does not follow from the fact that the common good concerns a great number or the majority while the individual good concerns only the individuals or a minority. It is not the numbers of even the generality in the quantitative sense but the intrinsicalness that determines the proper nature of the common good.[290]

The laity thus have as their proper field of endeavor the family and the State, and in this regard they have numerous rights and duties, for example, the natural right (and duty) to educate their children, and do not receive this from the State.

The common good of the Church is a different reality. This common good is the union of the soul with God in heaven when man enjoys the Beatific Vision. As this is a supernatural end, it can only be given by God who can alone establish the nature of the Church as a society and determine its authority. The laity are members of the Church by their baptismal consecration, which means that the end of the Church must also be the end of the laity, juxtaposed to and penetrating their living of the end of the family and the State.

In the family this end is easy to see because Christian marriage surpasses natural marriage in the type of love that the parties, as priests to one another, enjoy. Education in the Christian virtues, especially charity, becomes key. Also, as parents have a natural right and duty to pursue education in the natural virtues, so do they have the same rights regarding catechesis and charity. Catholic parents do not need a mandate from a diocesan catechetical office to teach their children the faith. They have a right and duty to do this by the very fact of their Christian marriage.

Two other interesting facts follow from this as well. The first is that an individual cannot oppose the Church to the State, arguing that citizenship in the State means one need (or ought) not embrace the moral order taught by the Church, lest this mix the ends of the two societies. Reason and faith supplement one another and cannot be inimical to one another. Thus, one cannot approve an action contrary to the Natural Law (e.g., abortion) by arguing that to oppose such an act—or worse, to argue that society has a right to it—would confuse Church and State. Since both the Church and the State are oriented to the common good of the same human nature, man realized in this world through justice is not inimical to man realized in the next through charity.

> But just as it must be recognized that the terrestrial city, rightly concerned with secular affairs, is governed by its own principles, thus also the ominous doctrine which seeks to build society with no regard for religion, and attacks and utterly destroys

the religious liberty of the citizens, is rightly to be rejected.[291]

Secondly, the rights and duties of the laity within the Church are quite extensive. The laity certainly have the right "to the word of God and the sacraments."[292] They also have a right to express their opinions. However, they have a corresponding duty of obedience, together with the clergy, to the authorities in the Church. This means that though there may be a legitimate right to dissent and express civil disobedience in the State, there is no such corresponding right in the Church. "Like all Christians, the laity should promptly accept in Christian obedience what is decided by the pastors, who, as teachers and rulers of the Church, represent Christ."[293]

Nor is this contrary to Christian freedom, as freedom is formed by the truth. When one is guided by the truth of God Himself, one cannot help but become more free. Vatican II ends the treatment of the ontological nature of the Church here. If all freely embrace the Gospel in obedience, then the laity will truly be a leaven in the world and this leaven, nourished by the clergy and religious life, will make the laity the soul of the world. "In a word: 'what the soul is in the body, let Christians be in the world.'"[294]

The soul is the animating force which guides and orders the body to pursue its perfection. Thus, Christians in all states of life will aid and support each other to pursue the perfection of the Church which is not its own existence, but rather the further perfections of union through holiness with God on earth, and, in heaven, through vision.

PART TWO
THE ACT OF THE CHURCH

CHAPTER SIX
The Universal Call To Holiness

Vatican II was the "Council of the Church," seeking to clarify the nature of the Church. In the first half of *Lumen Gentium*, chapters 1 through 4, the ontological nature of the being of the Church is explained. This procedure follows correct metaphysical methodology in which the nature of the thing is treated before its act is considered.

The nature of the Church is a society which is based in the social unity of the Persons of the Trinity in heaven. In light of this social union, all other aspects of the nature of the Church as a society follow: the divine origin and supernatural character of the Church, how the common priesthood of the faithful sets them apart from other religions, and the hierarchical nature of the Church respecting the stable order of the priesthood, with the Pope as head and bishops and priests, and the dignity of the Christian laity. This dignity must be exercised under the leadership of the hierarchy. In this section the great images of the People of God (respecting the Father in chapter 2) and the Mystical Body of Christ (respecting the Son in chapters 3 and 4) were treated.

The Council now takes up the act of the Church, or the reason the Church as a society exists. This reason is to sanctify the individual. The Church as a society exists to bring grace and holiness to the human race, not simply to perpetuate either its institutions or its power. Those earthly institutions and the power given by the sacraments are merely means to the end of holiness. The last four chapters of the document then take up the nature of that holiness, or the act of the Church, under the aspect of the third great image for the Church: Temple of the Holy Spirit—respecting the Holy Spirit.

Here one should note in passing that one cannot have a complete understanding of the Church without considering all three of these images, as this would be to separate off some of the Persons of the Trinity from others in God's society. Books, lectures and sermons since Vatican II have had a tendency to emphasize only the image of the People of God, out of context, as though it referred to the hierarchy or the mission of the Church. Many of these sources have suggested that the Church is now a democracy with nothing more than a mandate in this world to strive for world betterment. Laudable as world betterment might be, it is not the mission or purpose of the Church. The Church's true end is human interior perfection, which can only occur through the life of grace and can only be completed in the Vision of God in heaven. In fact, the *Catechism of the Catholic Church* very pointedly uses these images together as the foundation for its treatment of the Church. "The Church—People of God, Body of Christ, Temple of the Holy Spirit."[295]

In the order of the treatise, then, chapters 1 through 4 of *Lumen Gentium* examine the divine being and necessary social constitution of the Church. Chapters 5 through 8 examine the final cause, or purpose for which the Church as a society exists. "Further, after the exposition of the 'hierarchical constitution,' the document expressly turns its purpose to the 'end' intended by the Church [...]."[296]

"For this is the will of God, your sanctification." (1 Th. 4:3) Since the Church is a society reflecting the Holy Trinity and since it is founded not by men, but by Christ, it is "unfailingly holy."[297] Christ in fact, "willed and made it holy."[298] The purpose of this holy society is: "for the glory of God."[299] This is "its ontological and objective aspect and its end."[300]

As this is the nature and purpose of the Church, all of her members are called to the same grace and therefore to communion with the same Trinity. There are not, then, different communions or different grades of holiness in the Church as there are not different societies on earth which are the Church, different denominations or different trinities. There is only one Trinity and therefore only one Church in which all are called and given grace to have union with the same God. "It is therefore quite clear that all Christians in any state of life are called to the fullness of Christian life and to the perfection of love."[301]

The "spirituality of communion" which is at the basis of the society of the Church is practically and daily experienced in the communion with the Trinity in the life of the individual Christian. Each one is called to that communion and this is at the basis of the life of perfection of both the laity and religious. John Paul II has called the Church a "school of communion" and situated the development of this knowledge and love as the great challenge facing the Church in the 21ˢᵗ century.

> A spirituality of communion indicates above all the heart's contemplation of the mystery of the Trinity dwelling within us and whose light we must also be able to see shining on the faces of the brothers and sisters around us.[302]

Everyone in the Church has to pursue the complete perfection of the character of Baptism, by which they are conformed to Christ and experience an ontological communion with the Trinity. Everyone therefore is called to be holy according to his state in the Church. There are not several holinesses or several perfections, only one. Religious will be treated in a separate chapter, but each person in each vocation is called to a *life* of perfection, if not a *state* of perfection. The keystone of this life is communion in love with God or charity. "The charity of Christ is the source in us of all our merits before God."[303]

Bishops receive the communion with Christ offered in the Church as shepherds. Not only do they receive sacramental grace in ordination, but also the final perfection of the character of conformity to Christ as priest, prophet and king. The bishop shows his communion by teaching true doctrine and by his pastoral care for the faithful, especially seen in his solicitude to be the "moderator, promoter and guardian of her (the Church's) whole liturgical life."[304] Like the Good Shepherd, the bishop must lead with the staff, by doctrine, and offer the means of communion of grace by the rod of sacraments. The shepherd's rod is the extension of the power of his arm, as the sacraments are an extension of Christ's human nature, and the staff is the sign of the shepherd's office to direct the sheep, as the teaching of true doctrine directs the heart.

Priests also have the fullness of the character of Orders which allows them to consecrate the Eucharist and forgive sins. They are called to live perfection by offering their lives together with Christ on the altar, with a perfect giving of their whole selves. This is the source of the requirement of celibacy.

> The well-known German psychiatrist, Richard Krafft-Ebing, stated in his *Psychopathia Sexualis* (1886): "It shows a masterly psychological knowledge of

human nature that the Roman Catholic Church en-
joins celibacy upon its priests in order to emancipate
them from sensuality, and to concentrate their entire
activity in the pursuit of their calling."[305]

The faithful offer the sacrifice of the Mass, but through the
intermediary of the human priest, and not in the strict sense. As the
human ministerial priest does offer in the strict sense, he must completely identify his whole love with the same love Christ has for the
Church in making the offering of the Cross. When he says, "This is
my Body" and "This is my Blood" as he acts in the person of Christ,
all his affective life must be completely taken up with Christ. It is
not the assembly who gathers and consecrates with the priest acting
in their name. Rather the priest offers in the name of Christ and the
people participate.

> Nor is the Eucharistic Sacrifice to be considered
> a "concelebration," in the univocal sense, of the
> Priest along with the people who are present. On
> the contrary, the Eucharist celebrated by the Priests
> "is a gift which radically transcends the power of
> the community [...] The community that gathers
> for the celebration absolutely requires an ordained
> priest, who presides over it so that it may be truly
> a Eucharistic convocation. On the other hand, the
> community is by itself incapable of providing an
> ordained minister." [...] [T]erms such as "celebrat-
> ing community" or "celebrating assembly" [...] and
> similar terms should not be used injudiciously.[306]

The hardships of the priesthood should drive priests on to a deeper
communion with the crucified Lord who offered his life for us. "They
have the duty to pray and offer sacrifice for their people and for the
whole People of God, appreciating what they do and imitating what
they touch with their hands."[307]

The prayer of priests should be filled with the vertical communion
of life in which the Church is plunged into the life of the Trinity. The
Mass is the principal place where this is true, but also the Liturgy of
the Hours as an extension of the Mass is a powerful implementation
of the duty of the priests to pray for their people. "Priests as well as

deacons aspiring to the priesthood are obliged to fulfill the liturgy of the hours in accordance with the proper liturgical books."[308] "The obligation of clerics to pray the Divine Office daily is canonically and juridically imposed. This duty, incumbent upon all clergy in major orders, derives from "ancient tradition and immemorial custom [...].""[309] The same solicitude of priests for holiness should animate those who participate in some way in the actions of the priest, either as a part of them like the deacon, or in preparation like the seminarian.

All the vocations, whether marriage, widowhood, the single life, the priesthood or the religious life, should be characterized by an active pursuit of the virtues and charity.

> Opportunities for the practice of fortitude, magnanimity, and magnificence do not often occur; but gentleness, moderation, integrity, and humility are virtues with which all the actions of our lives should be colored. There are virtues nobler than these; but the practice of these is more necessary.[310]

Some believe if they are not priests or religious they are excused from a life of the virtues and contemplation. The fact that grace is an ontological communion with the Trinity argues against this. The duties and joy which the love of grace imposes can be found in every situation and every walk of life.

> Among the virtues we should prefer that which suits our duty best, and not that which is most to our taste and, although everyone ought to have all the virtues, yet not everyone is bound to practice them to the same extent. Each ought to give himself especially to those which are required by the kind of life to which he is called.[311]

The nature of grace and the resulting call to holiness make it clear that holiness is not a question of methods or external settings. Indeed, the external setting in which holiness is pursued is of relative indifference. One can even find grace or holiness in a concentration camp.

> One of the French priests imprisoned in the concentration camp of Buchenwald once said, "When

one speaks of the privilege to have come out alive from Buchenwald, one also should consider the fact that it has been a greater privilege to have been sent there, and even this, without the first is a privilege indeed.

Yes, it has been a privilege, even though in the beginning I rebelled against God's holy will, and in my conceit demanded an answer as to why it had to be me and not my neighbor who had to undergo such misery. But as time passed, my eyes were opened, and I began to see what before I could not comprehend. [...] but now in prison I realized that I could not live without Him (God)—that life without God has no meaning.

Buchenwald was a hard and bitter experience, but it was an advantage to those who know how to profit from it. Why does God permit wars and concentration camps? Again the answer is simple: because He loves us, because He wants to bring back to His fold those who otherwise in a life of pleasure and lusts would have been lost.[312]

So, the life of charity is the life of perfection. There can be no second-class Christians because charity is the direct result of the personal experience of the union which sanctifying grace gives us. Charity is a divine gift because it is an infused virtue. Living the commandments by which we avoid sin is not sufficient for enjoying the communion with God which charity offers to all.

Christ added counsels of perfection to the commandments. Individuals are asked to give up legitimate goods in these counsels so they may preserve the communion with God which grace offers us. Traditionally, these counsels are three: poverty, chastity and obedience. These are the cure to the desire for domination which each of us experiences as a result of the Original Sin. Though we experience this weakness as the three lusts: lust of the eyes, lust of the flesh and the pride of life (1 John 2:16), they can all be reduced to our desire to dominate and manipulate others to our own wills. "For him (Augustine), the over-riding tendency to iniquity was that powerful substitute for sex which is the peculiar prerogative of the spiritually minded, the 'desire to dominate.'"[313] Poverty is the remedy for the lust of the eyes; chastity for the lust of the flesh; and obedience for the pride of life. All Christians must embrace the counsels, but not as a fixed mode of life. Religious do this as a fixed mode of life, others according to what their state of life allows.

> Renunciation of one's possessions may be considered in two ways. First, as being actual: and thus it is not essential, but a means to perfection [...] Hence nothing hinders the state of perfection from being without renunciation of one's possessions, and the same applies to other outward practices. Secondly, it may be considered in relation to one's preparedness, in the sense of being prepared to renounce and give away all: and this belongs directly to perfection.[314]

The preservation and advancement of the life of charity is the duty and joy of every Christian and the place where the perfection of the Church as a supernatural society is most clearly lived. This is not easy, and demands constant surrender to God of our desires to dominate. This is done through the virtues and the gifts which correspond to grace and are preserved in the living the counsels according to the way of life one has. In every sense of the word, this is a combat. This combat, and the call to holiness which underlies it, are the basis for the progress in the life of prayer.

> Prayer is both a gift of grace and a determined response on our part. It always presupposes effort. [...] Prayer is a battle. Against whom? Against ourselves and against the wiles of the tempter who does all he can to turn man away from prayer, from union with God. [...] The "spiritual battle" of the Christian's new life is inseparable from the battle of prayer.[315]

So, the act of the Church is solidly based on the grace which is given to each Christian in Baptism. The reason the hierarchy exists, the priests preach and celebrate Mass, and the whole sacramental order was founded, was to aid in the increasing healing which grace brings us. Grace is the seed of the whole organism of the virtues and the gifts. There are not two perfections, because the same seed is given to everyone, an ontological share in the very life of the Trinity. It is this seed which is the source of the universal call to holiness.

CHAPTER SEVEN
Consecrated Life

There was a long debate in Vatican II as to whether religious life should be treated in one chapter with the universal call to holiness or treated in a separate chapter. Though all of the Fathers wanted to emphasize that holiness in the Church is one because grace in the Church is one, they also affirmed that there were different vocations to living the same holiness. To understand the special place of religious life in the action of the Church, it is useful to consider the discussion which occurred among the Fathers at Vatican II.

Those who favored two chapters made several points. Putting religious life together with the universal call to holiness, they argued, obfuscates the unique contribution of religious. Just as in the first half of the Constitution, the general nature of the Church is treated before the distinction between the hierarchy and the laity, so, regarding holiness, it is better to treat of the general nature of holiness and then of specific states, especially the state of the counsels of perfection. The laity procure the consecration of the world by their presence in it and in a private way. Religious procure this consecration in a public sense.

To treat religious life in one chapter with holiness might give the impression that the state and life of religious are incidental to the Church. Ecumenically this would make no sense if one sought reunion with the Eastern Church, where monasticism has always been held in great esteem. Though religious life is not a state relating to the hierarchical constitution, the public witness it involves is necessary for the action of the Church in pursuing heaven.

Some contemporary religious would seem to justify this fear of the Fathers at Vatican II, because they themselves seem to think that religious life is accidental to the existence of the Church. As one sister theologian put it, "The Spirit is calling religious to something. Maybe to end religious life. But that's not a foregone conclusion."[316]

Christ in fact both established and recommended the state of perfection. The Church still teaches that the state of virginity is a more perfect state. "The Church has always taught the pre-eminence of perfect chastity for the sake of the Kingdom, and rightly considers it the 'door' of the whole consecrated life."[317] Though it is true the state of virginity is counseled for perfection in charity, it is nonetheless an essential state for the perfection of the Church in pursuing the end for which the structure exists, which is holiness. The religious life, (or the "consecrated life," as this term more corresponds to some modern ways of living the counsels even without public vows) is not a distinct vocation in regard to the hierarchy of the Church, its *esse*. It is rather a distinct vocation regarding the action of the Church as a spiritual society, its *operari* or act.

The religious life was founded by Christ in the gospels and exists as a seed in actions which are brought into full development in the various monastic movements, beginning with the Fathers of the desert. Besides the difference in the Church between hierarchy and laity, there is also that difference which is drawn between those who are called to public witness of the counsels of perfection, and others. Some of the Council Fathers felt that two chapters would emphasize this difference.

Those who favored one chapter did so because there was an opinion which some people held in the Church, that the only individuals called to perfection in the Church were religious. This had caused a great laxity in spiritual life; for the laity did not aspire to contemplative prayer. The Council Fathers thought religious life should be something seen not so much as juridical division but as a charismatic sign giving witness to the increase of charity in the whole community. They did not want religious to seem to constitute a kind of spiritual "aristocracy," or to seem to be divided from the Church as a whole, as though they were above it or possessed some special Gnostic experience of truth not shared by Christians in general. In fact, religious have the *munus significandi et testificandi* (mission of being a sign and a witness) which some Fathers believed would be better served if religious were treated in one chapter with holiness.

The Council chose to treat religious in a separate chapter, to emphasize the special nature of the religious vocation. This vocation is in a separate place than that of the distinction of the hierarchy. This place is the complete living of the life of Baptism here on earth. It is also a sign of what the life of heaven will be like where "they neither marry nor are given in marriage." (Matt. 22:30)

To understand this place, one must first understand the reason for the evangelical counsels. Though in Baptism each man received back sanctifying grace which was lost in the Original Sin, no one received back the special, preternatural gifts given to Adam and Eve before the Fall. As a result, baptized Christians live the life of grace in struggle. The traditional three areas of struggle are the famous three lusts enumerated in 1 John 2: 16, "For all that is in the world, the lust of the flesh, the lust of the eyes and the pride of life is not from the Father but from the world."

Though Christ gave us back grace in the redemption, we did not receive back the complete integrity of the state of Adam before the Original Sin. Thus, each Christian now struggles not only with sin, but also with the lack of purity of intention which too much concentration on even good things of this world can hinder. The commandments oblige everyone. By them, all are required to renounce evil acts. But in the New Testament, Christ invited all to surrender their attachment to even good things, insofar as these things would hinder divine love or charity.

> Besides its precepts, the New Law also includes the evangelical counsels. The traditional distinction between God's commandments and the evangelical counsels is drawn in relation to charity, the perfection of Christian life. The precepts are intended to remove whatever is incompatible with charity. The aim of the counsels is to remove whatever might hinder the development of charity, even if it is not contrary to it.[318]

All are obliged to the counsels, but not in a permanent, fixed manner of living. Because religious have received a grace from God, a special consecration, they are obliged to the counsels all the time and renounce even legitimate goods that they may be more occupied with love of God and service to his Church. This invitation is by the will of Christ. Though there are many different manners of life approved by the Church as legitimate stable forms by which a Catholic may legitimately live the life of Christ, Christ is the one who instituted

religious life, not the Church. The Church approves juridical forms
of life as consonant with Christ's call, but not the call itself. "The
teaching and example of Christ provide the foundation for the evangelical counsels of chaste self-dedication to God, of poverty and of
obedience. The Apostles and Fathers of the Church commend them,
as so do her doctors and pastors. They therefore constitute a gift of
God which the Church has received from her Lord and which by his
grace she always safeguards."[319]

The religious life is not some middle ground in the hierarchical
structure of the Church between clergy and laity. Yet, it is necessary
to the existence of the Church, and not just an accidental historical
accretion. "This form of life has its own place in relation to the divine
and hierarchical structure of the Church. Not, however, as though it
were a middle way [...]."[320] The religious life is not, then, necessary
for the structure of the Church as a hierarchical society, and so it is
not treated in the part of the document *Lumen Gentium* dealing with
the being of the Church. The necessity of religious or consecrated
life relates to the mission of the Church to witness to the human
integration of holiness and to prepare for heaven. Christ invited us
to the counsels that nothing might hinder our love for God on earth
as a final cause. "The state of life, then, which is constituted by the
profession of the evangelical counsels, while not entering into the
hierarchical structure of the Church, belongs undeniably to her life
and holiness."[321]

The purpose of consecrated life is to serve as a witness and example to the freedom and service which charity brings to man. This is
why it is called a state of perfection. "If however, someone obliged his
whole life by a vow to God so that he should diligently serve him in
works of perfection, he at once assumes simply speaking the condition
or state of perfection."[322] This is not say that religious are absolutely
perfect. This belongs only to God. Nor do they experience perfect
charity in the sense that all they do is actually referred to God. Such
charity was not possible in this life to anyone but Christ and Mary.
Rather, religious wish habitually to refer their whole lives to God by
voluntarily surrendering even very good things because our weakness
regarding them threatens the perfect freedom of charity.

Religious life must be seen as a special grace given by God to
the person, freely entered into, embraced not because one considers

the goods surrendered to be evil. It must also be seen generally as a charism in the Church, embraced according to constitutions or laws approved by the hierarchy. Both clerics and laity can place themselves under this special consecration. "[H]e desires to derive still more abundant fruit from the grace of his baptism. For this purpose he makes profession in the Church of the evangelical counsels. He does so for two reasons: first, in order to be set free from hindrances that could hold him back from fervent charity and perfect worship of God, and secondly, in order to consecrate himself in a more thoroughgoing way to the service of God."[323]

Since the basis for the society of the whole Church is communion with the Trinity, a consecrated person embraces that communion with a special and unique obligation in the Church. "Consecrated persons are asked to be true experts of communion, and to practice its spirituality as witnesses and artisans of that plan of communion which stands at the center of history according to God."[324] Pope John Paul II has defined the spirituality of communion as involving both inner union with the Trinity and exterior action on behalf of the Church. "A spirituality of communion indicates above all the heart's contemplation of the mystery of the Trinity dwelling within us and whose light we must also be able to see shining on the faces of the brothers and sisters around us."[325]

The life of consecration was established by Christ for many reasons. This life imitates a sacrificial holocaust when, by perpetual vows, religious give themselves completely to Christ. Thus, it involves God-centered worship. This is why vows are fittingly pronounced in the context of the Eucharist. This state has an ecclesiological and apostolic aspect, as the inner communion with the Trinity must be expressed in exterior communion with the Church and service of the members of Christ's Mystical Body. The life also has a Christological and eschatological aspect, as it is the life Christ lived, and looks forward, as a sign, to the future life of the resurrection where they "neither marry nor are given in marriage." Religious life does not stand between the life of the laity and that of the clergy. Rather, religious consecration stands in the middle of the two states of innocence and glory. The call of Christ to address "hardness of heart" is addressed to the man of concupiscence who has grace but finds it difficult to live the life of grace. The purpose of this life is shown in the Preface for Virgins and Religious which states that consecrated life "recalls mankind to its first innocence and invites us to taste on earth of the gifts of the world to come."[326]

There is a twofold dimension which must be preserved in the life of the counsels. First, the Church must respect the charisma of religious founders, and the hierarchy should not unduly interfere in the manner in which religious live their lives. But coupled with this, it must be affirmed that as religious life involves ways of life and charisms approved by the hierarchy, so no religious institute is above the Church, especially the Pope. Indeed, the primary superior of every religious order is the Pope, who sanctions the fact that the superiors of a given institute have the right to demand obedience from their members. "Institutes of consecrated life, since they are dedicated in a special way to the service of God and the whole Church, are in a particular manner subject to its supreme authority. The individual members are bound to obey the Supreme Pontiff as their highest superior, by reason also of their sacred bond of obedience."[327]

The consecrated life involves two principles, both of which must be affirmed: the life must be voluntary, and it must be supernaturally oriented. "There are eunuchs who have made themselves so for the sake of the kingdom of heaven." The first part of this statement of the Lord shows the voluntary character, and the second the supernatural purpose. In renouncing material goods (lust of the eyes); sexual experience (lust of the flesh) and choice over one's life (obedience), the religious is seeking to live a life integrated in communion with the Trinity in charity. One does not therefore deny these basic goods as goods, but surrenders them for something better, i.e., the complete freedom of the personality, based on acquiring a supernatural attitude towards creation. One desires to know as God knows, and to love as God loves while on earth. The vows are not ends in themselves, but means to this perfect freedom. Therefore, embracing them does not involve frustration of the human personality, but its final liberty, provided vows are made for the right reasons.

In fact, the vows address our tendencies to domination and manipulation of others. Without the complete healing of grace, Christians still have a tendency to fall back on material goods as the remedy to the problems that perennially beset mankind. One who cannot submit to the providence of God, seeks to govern the world by his own providence, even to expense of the good of others. This is really what lust is all about: the will to power. What one is addressing in the renunciation demanded by the vows is this desire to dominate, and embracing the desire to allow God to direct our life again in all our loves.

Were one to surrender material goods from the idea that he could not make a living, or sexuality because he hated the whole idea of the opposite sex (or worse feared them), or choice over one's life because he wanted to remain a perpetual teenager, this would not serve. This really would frustrate the personality.

> At the same time let all realize that while the profession of the evangelical counsels involves the renunciation of goods that undoubtedly deserve to be highly valued, it does not constitute an obstacle to the true development of the human person but by its nature is supremely beneficial to that development.[328]

The two points are essential then: freedom and a supernatural attitude. "Pius XII teaches that religious life is not a refuge of safety given to those who are fearful or anxious, but demands a great spirit and zeal for giving oneself [...]."[329] This is because of the supernatural orientation of the human spirit which because of the presence of the intellect can be satisfied with nothing less than heaven. It is heaven and our orientation there which sets us free to live a complete and integrated life on earth. Those who are called by God and embrace religious vows in this way, relying on grace and not on self, cannot become truncated human beings. Men in vows cannot become less masculine than men without vows or women in vows less feminine than women without vows. They should be more.

The virginal male and female do not renounce spousal love in itself, but spousal love after the manner of this world. They do not renounce paternity and maternity in itself but a paternity and maternity of one family after the manner of this world. They are to become spiritual fathers of all and spiritual mothers of all. This obviously can only be accomplished by surrendering to grace, not by nature.

As this is a state which hearkens back to the way Adam was before the Original Sin, and looks forward to how man will be in the state of glory in heaven, it cannot be lived in any other way than with constant prayer and a supernatural attitude.

> For the counsels, when willingly embraced in accordance with each one's personal vocation, contribute in so small degree to the purification of the heart and to spiritual freedom: they continually stimulate one to ardour in the life of love.[330]

CHAPTER EIGHT
The Pilgrim Church

The concept of the Church as *viator* or pilgrim has caused much difficulty in the post-Vatican II Church. This is odd, as the difficulty seems to rest on a fundamental misunderstanding of why this chapter was included in the document and what the concept of "pilgrim" means. Many have interpreted this term, and the concept, to signify that there is something fundamentally evolving about the structure of the Church as a society. In this view, the Church would be continually deconstructing and reconstructing her means for implementing authority according to the "spirit of the age." This would suggest that she came unfinished from the hands of her Master, Christ, and further, that the structure of the episcopacy or the papacy could evolve into some whole new model of authority completely different from what it had been in the past.

Some people reflect this point by appealing to the concept of the evolution of dogma, forgetting that evolution must always be homogeneous and not heterogeneous. The Church can only deepen in its self-understanding of institutions received from the Lord. The manner of authority and the sacraments may evolve in understanding, but not so as to contradict our previous way of understanding them. One could not decide, for example, that there should only be four sacraments based on evolution of dogma. Instead, evolution builds on previous truths and practices and makes clearer how they relate to Christ.

"This Chapter (Seven) was introduced according to the will of Pope John XXIII [...]."[331] The complete title of the chapter demonstrates the doctrine taught here: "On the eschatological constitution of the pilgrim Church and her union with the heavenly Church."[332] The Church only finds its final fulfillment in the communion of saints in heaven, but this does not mean that one is dealing with two substantially different societies in the earthly and heavenly Church. In fact, they are one and the same society. They are related as imperfectly fulfilled to perfectly fulfilled. The pilgrim Church is relatively perfect according to the manner of this world, as it has all the means

necessary to attain its ultimate end. It is not absolutely perfect except
in the communion of saints in heaven.

The point of this chapter perfectly corresponds to the beginning
of the document, where the Church was examined as a mystery. The
problem is that in the post-Vatican II Church, the whole question of
eschatology has become very confused. Cardinal Ratzinger pointed
out in an address he gave to European theologians in 1989, that some
theologians in the post-Vatican II Church have not only denied hell
and purgatory, but also the existence of heaven. Many theologians now
teach that the Church looks for its perfection in a human future, but
not one which is outside this world. When this fact is used to interpret
the concept of a Pilgrim Church, many take it to mean that through
democratic evolution of structures corresponding to the "spirit of the
age," the Church will be realized as the perfect society here on earth
through some egalitarian optimism.

Actually, the reflection on the Church as pilgrim underlines the
connection between the hierarchical and sacramental earthly Church
and the heavenly communion of saints. "The Church, to which we are
all called in Christ Jesus, and in which by the grace of God we acquire
holiness, will receive its perfection only in the glory of heaven, when
will come the time of the renewal of all things."[333]

This answers an idea that there will be some realized future here
in this world where there will be a further revelation of the Holy Spirit
than the one in Christ, who established the physical Church of the
hierarchy and sacraments on Pentecost. This spiritual Church will be
more perfect than the present one and will be a Church without structure or required sacraments. According to this idea, there were three
ages in the history of the world. The first was the age of the Father,
which is the Old Testament. The second was the age of the Son, which
is the New Testament. This would be succeeded by a new and more
perfect age here on earth, the age of the Spirit. The characteristics of
this age would be that there would no more physical mediators, and
man would experience a direct inspiration of the Holy Spirit which
would teach a Gnostic knowledge, not open to definition or judgment
of any Church organ.

St. Thomas answered this idea by explaining that there are indeed
three ages of the world. The first is indeed the Old Testament, which

is the age of both the Father and the Son, realized only with the coming the Messiah. The second age is the New Testament, which is the age of the Son and the Holy Spirit, because it is only complete when the Son sends—and continually sends—the Holy Spirit to reside in his Church. This is the Church of the complete revelation, here on earth, of the Trinity in Word and Sacrament. The place of the hierarchy is necessary for this as the servant of the Word and the givers of the sacraments. This will be succeeded by a new and more perfect, third age, but this will be the heavenly Church when we shall see the Beatific Vision.

> The Old Law was not only of the Father, but also of the Son: because Christ was prefigured in the Old Law. Thus the Lord says: "If you believed Moses, you would perhaps also believe in me, for he wrote about me." (John 5:46) Likewise the New Law is not only about Christ, but also about the Holy Spirit according to Romans 8:2: "The Law of the Spirit of life in Christ Jesus, etc." So another law should not be expected which is of the Holy Spirit.[334]

The Church proclaims that the future life is begun here, through grace and holiness. So, the renewal of the world which is an interior renewal of grace in the heart is the beginning on earth of the process that will only end in heaven by vision. This is the meaning of "realized eschatology." Worship and morals are the manner in which heaven is to be realized on earth. Regarding worship, the sacraments and especially the Blessed Sacrament are not a celebration of our earthly community which we create, but an engraced elevation in which we participate in the worship of heaven. "It is in this eternal liturgy that the Spirit and the Church enable us to participate whenever we celebrate the mystery of salvation in the sacraments."[335]

This worship supports our living the moral life which gives us a "sanctity which is real though imperfect."[336] Francis de Sales advises, "[...] [T]o be in this world and not to feel these stirrings of passion—these two things are incompatible. [...] [I]t is heresy to claim that we can persist in the same state here on earth, inasmuch as the Holy Spirit, speaking of human beings through Job, has declared that we are never in the same state."[337]

The vision of God must be the perfection of the society of the Church, because only in this vision are both the desire of the intellect to know the truth and the desire of the will to love stilled. Only the vision of God can bring this about, because of the potential of the intellect to know the first cause of the world. Man's free acts are ordered to this perfection; which is also called beatitude. This beatitude is begun here by the love of the will in charity elevated to partake of divine nature, but can only be completed in heaven through vision. The Church contains the final perfect revelation of the society of the Trinity which one could have here on earth, but that same society is only perfectly experienced in the final society of heaven, where there will be no mixture of imperfection or possibility of sin.

> The formal constituent of beatitude is indeed the intellect's vision of the divine essence: the order of predication. But the will's union with the supreme good is more concretely comprehensive, indeed it is the measure of the different degrees of the vision as we see in *Summa contra Gentiles*, III, 59: the order of causality. Does not St. Thomas in *Summa contra Gentiles* III, 62 hold that some admiration remains even in heaven and that this is the reason for the will's indefectibility in beatitude?[338]

Both experiences are part of the same society, as they both participate in the same Trinity. "In paragraph 49 and the following it is provided that the text should show the ultimate doctrinal foundation of the whole Chapter, namely that the earthly and heavenly Church make up one People of God and one Mystical Body of Jesus Christ."[339] Christ is head of his whole Mystical Body which includes those who enjoy communion with the Trinity by vision in heaven, those who enjoy communion with the Trinity by faith and charity realized in Purgatory, and those who enjoy communion with the Trinity by faith and charity not yet completely realized in the Church here on earth. All these members are in touch with one another and influence each other through a union of charity. "All of us, however, in varying degrees and in different ways, share in the same charity towards God and our neighbors, and we all sing the one hymn of glory to our God."[340]

The communion of saints is based on the communion in the Trinity, and one cannot have a complete understanding of the Church as a society without reference to this. The invocation of the saints, then, is not an attempt to replace communion with the Trinity through Christ, but to recognize that by the communion of love, all the members of the Church relate to one another. The saints are invoked, and prayers are offered for the dead, by the Church on earth so that the saints may encourage and support us on our journey towards God, and we who can still perform meritorious acts may influence the purgation of those in Purgatory who cannot. The communion of friendship in Christ is therefore the basis for these truths about the Church.

> If we speak of happiness in the present life [...] the happy man needs friends, but not because of usefulness, because he is sufficient in himself; nor because of delight, because he has perfect delight in himself in the work of virtue; but because of good action. He does good to them, he delights in seeing them do good and in turn they aid him and do good to him. [...] But if we speak of the perfect happiness of heaven, the fellowship of friends is not strictly necessary for beatitude [...] but as enhancing our happiness.[341]

Vatican II meant to explain the exact place of devotion to the saints from an ecumenical intention. The Fathers meant to draw a middle ground between an excessive devotion to the saints, as though they were venerated apart from love for Christ and as rivals to him, and a defect of those who fail to venerate them at all. Instead, the doctrine of the pilgrim Church emphatically places the Church as sacrament in relief, and underlines that it is a divine society with a supernatural purpose which forms the union of all its members. The Council's ecumenical intention was clearly to state that "the cult of the saints differs essentially from the cult of *latria* which is the offering due to God alone."[342]

This communion is clearly seen in the participation which the members of the earthly Church have in the heavenly liturgy. One text already cited explains how this worship is reflected in all the sacraments. This is especially true of the Eucharist. "It is especially in the sacred liturgy that our union with the heavenly Church is best realized; [...] When, then, we celebrate the Eucharistic sacrifice we are most closely united to the worship of the heavenly Church

[…]."[343] This union is shown in the fact that the union of the saints in our worship is invoked in the Mass, in the Preface and also in the Eucharistic Prayer. St. Thomas Aquinas demonstrates that it is the same Christ in his body, blood, soul and divinity who is worshipped on the altar and in heaven, by placing the words of the Wedding Song of the Lamb (Rev. 5: 11-13), the text with which chapter 7 of *Lumen Gentium* ends,[344] in the last verse of the hymn *Tantum Ergo*.

> *Genitori genitoque*
> *Laus et iubilatio*
> *Salus, honor, virtus quoque*
> *Sit et benedictio*
> *Procedenti ab utroque*
> *Compar sit laudatio.*

> To the Father and the Son
> Praise and glory,
> Blessing and honor and
> Glory and might be
> Equally to the Holy Spirit.

CHAPTER NINE
The Blessed Virgin Mary

There was a long debate during Vatican II as to whether Our Lady should be treated in a single document or placed within the document on the Church. The Fathers decided to place the document on the Virgin Mary within the document on the Church.

> And finally in Chapter VIII special consideration is given to the Blessed Virgin Mary, both in the mystery of Christ, whose mother she is, and in the mystery of the Church whose maternal and virginal type she is. In this final chapter, in the form of a final flourish, the whole exposition about the mystery of the Church is recapitulated.[345]

The importance of Mary as the motherly and virginal type of the Church because she is the Mother of God cannot be underestimated. In her we see the summit and explanation of what it means to be a member of the Church. If anyone should claim that because the Catholic Church is made up of sinners that the means of salvation are not with her, one need only point to Mary to show these means are sufficient. "For in the mystery of the Church, which is itself rightly called mother and virgin, the Blessed Virgin stands out in eminent and singular fashion as exemplar of both virgin and mother."[346]

Mary as Virgin and Mother is intimately the personal model of the Church which as a society is a Virgin and Mother. The Church is mother because she communicates grace in the sacraments; she is virgin in the purity of her faith, communicated through the ministry of the Word by doctrine. Both doctrine and sacraments are the foundation of the continual sharing in the life of the Trinity by sanctifying grace.

Since the Church is a communion with the Trinity, the "singular dignity of the God-bearer (Mary) is evident from her contact with the divine Persons themselves."[347] This contact gives rise to Mary's unique place in the Church as the first and most prominent member, and also is the foundation of the four Marian dogmas defined by the Church:

her Divine Motherhood as *Theotokos* and New Eve; her Perpetual
Virginity; her Immaculate Conception; and her Assumption.

The primary mystery of Mary is her divine motherhood. It is
from this that all the other mysteries flow. "Likewise she is mother,
namely according to the flesh of Christ himself, but also mother of
his brethren by her spiritual cooperation."[348] In treating the mystery of
Mary as a chapter in the document on the Church, the Council Fathers
in no way wanted to denigrate her participation in the Redemption.
Quite the contrary. They wanted to underscore her *munus* or office in
the Church more. "Wherefore she is hailed as a pre-eminent and as a
wholly unique member of the Church, and as its type and outstanding model in faith and charity."[349] This is because she is endowed
"with the high office and dignity of the Mother of the Son of God,
and therefore she is also the beloved daughter of the Father and the
temple of the Holy Spirit."[350]

Mary is the new Eve, because like the first virgin mother of the
human race, she received a message from an angel. In her Annuncia-
tion, that message was an invitation to loving obedient cooperation in
the divine plan. The angel is like the priest who witnesses the heavenly
nuptials between the Virgin and God. God has already given his consent to the marriage and therefore the conception. Now, Mary in our
name is asked to give hers. She exemplifies the human cooperation of
the whole Church in receiving faith and grace in her catechesis and
her loving obedience. She conceives the Word, in faith, in her mind
and then in her body. She is therefore the Mother of God because in
her the Person of the Word took a human nature.

This mystery was rejected by Nestorius who maintained that
Mary could be called the Mother of Christ, but not really the Mother
of God. His idea has been characterized as leading to the idea that
there are two persons in Christ, one divine and one human. God
dwelt in man in Christ, as a man dwells in a house, without any substantial connection between the two. In other words, the two natures
of Christ were so distinct that they led to two different persons that
enjoy a union in Christ like our union with God by grace. Instead,
the Church maintains that there is a distinction between person (the
radical individual) and nature (the principles enjoyed by the radical
individual). In Christ, the person of the Word who enjoys a definite
nature took other principles to himself to also act as a person, a human

nature. This is not an accidental union like grace in us, but a personal union which is unique.

The heresy of Nestorius denied this personal union. His heresy tends to adoptionism, the idea that the grace of God in Christ is just like the grace of Christ in us, that of an adopted and not a natural son. This position was rejected at the Council of Ephesus which used the word "God-bearer" (*theotokos, Dei Genitrix*) of Mary.

Many today would like to reduce Christ to merely a good man who was somehow identified with God, who only pre-existed his conception in the womb of Mary in the Father's intention. Others would see some distinction between the Jesus of faith and the Jesus of history, or Christology from above (the dogmas of faith) and a Christology from below (the Jesus sensibly experienced by the Apostles). This distinction is based on an old problem which has its origin in the philosophy of Emmanuel Kant. Kant sought to reform thinking by teaching that nothing metaphysical could be derived from the senses; the metaphysical could only be derived from the subject's need. The Jesus of history is the one described by the senses. The Jesus of faith is the one described by the subject's need.

Catholicism knows no such distinction. Metaphysical knowledge can be arrived at through the senses and so the Jesus of faith and history are the same. Mary, then, is a maternal type because she gave birth to the Person of the Word, but in his human nature. The cooperation of her faith was necessary for the experience of motherhood because the inner union of spousal love (her faith, charity and obedience) were so strong that they brought forth Jesus in the flesh. So no "*discrepancy should appear* [it. orig.] between the woman, the Mother of Christ in the Gospels, and the figure of the Blessed Virgin just as it is treated in the theological tract and cherished by the Christian people."[351]

Mary is the Mother of the Word and so, by her believing, is the prime analogate for faith and the obedience which cooperates with grace in faith. As the Mother, she is intimately associated with all the mysteries of the life of her Son.

In her Annuciation, Mary as the new Eve, consents in the name of the human race to be the vessel of grace and bring forth the one who fulfills the first prophecy of the Redemption, in Genesis 3: 15: "I will put enmity between you and the woman, and between your offspring and hers; he will strike your head and you will strike his heel."

In her Visitation, she as the New Ark of the Covenant, brings the Covenant, Jesus to perform an act of ordinary charity to Elizabeth. Thus, she is the image of the active life. John the Baptist dances in the womb as he is cleansed from Original Sin in recognizing Christ, and Mary, in her Magnificat, evangelizes us in the mercy God has shown his people. Radical feminists have changed the Magnificat into a prayer of Mary addressed to God by altering pronouns to avoid saying "He" of God. Instead in the Gospel text, Mary evangelizes Elizabeth and is the first catechist in the true faith.

In the Nativity, Joseph plays the midwife. The shepherds brought by angels believe in Christ, representing the Jews and the uneducated. The Magi represent the Gentiles and the educated, brought by nature, in the star, to believe. In both cases, they find the child "with his mother."

In the Presentation in the Temple, Mary brings the Lord of the Temple to meet the Temple. The New Law comes to meet and fulfill the Old Law. Simeon addresses his words concerning his own death and faith in Christ the Redeemer, the "glory of Israel and the light of the Gentiles" to Mary as well. He then pronounces a prophecy concerning both Christ and his mother Mary.

In the Finding in the Temple, Christ demonstrates his position as the prime teacher of Israel. He does not remonstrate with Mary and Joseph, but asks them why they sought him *for three days.* Where else would he be but in his Father's house? Mary, as the image of contemplation, keeps all these things and treasures them in her heart as a model to us of the necessity of constant meditation on the life of her Son.

During Jesus' public life at Cana, Mary is the image of the intercessory prayer of the Church. His disciples believe in him as a result of an action done at her behest. Christ says that his Mother and brothers are those who hear the Word of God and keep it. This is not a denigration of Mary, but an exaltation of her because she is the one who hears the Word within and keeps it *par excellence.*

In the Passion and on the Cross, Mary offers her life with Christ's so she is completely associated with his redemptive obedience and

love. She lovingly consents to his offering and so is given to us, the
ones won for his Church by this offering, to be our Mother. She shows
this motherhood because after his Ascension, she participates with
the Church praying in the Upper Room, in the first novena, for the
coming of the Holy Spirit.

Mary is a type of the Church in her virginity, which is not only
a virginity of body, but also of mind. "The deepening faith in the
virginal motherhood led the Church to confess Mary's real and
perpetual virginity even in the act of giving birth to the Son of God
made man."[352] The perpetual virginity of Mary has been seriously
questioned today by those who miss the point of her spiritual connection with the Church. Her virginity of heart is seen "in faith, and
obedience, fidelity and charity."[353] Her purity within is shown in her
faith because she believes in the fullness of the mystery of her Son.
The Church imitates that purity in teaching the complete faith and
all the articles of the Creed. Her faith is the prototype for that faith
and so she is the "hammer of heretics." She shows this purity in the
obedience of her will, an obedience which is never wanting because
she is always "full of grace."

Since Mary is the Mother of Christ, and a virgin in heart as well
as in body, God gave her special privileges which fittingly correspond
to these mysteries. In her inception as a person, she is immaculately
conceived. In her passing from the world, she does not experience
the corruption of death, but by a unique privilege is assumed into
heaven with her body.

The Immaculate Conception is central to the mystery of Mary as
Mother and Virgin. As Mother of God, she should be untouched by
sin. So, God chose to keep Original Sin from touching her body and
soul, so that she might be a fit Mother for the Word. However, this
privilege was not given her apart from her relationship with Christ
the Redeemer. Rather, since she occupies first place among the redeemed, this gift is given to her precisely because of her connection
to the cross of Christ. She is also preserved from all actual sins and
from temptation so that the virginity of her soul may correspond to
the virginity of her body.

Her obedience is therefore completely spontaneous. She has no
concupiscence to compromise her inner union with God. All virtues

and gifts are given to her, and she is the example of all these to the members of the rest of the Church.

In the end of her life, she is also presented to the Church as a sign of the perfection of the life of the Church in heaven. So she is an eschatological icon of the Church.[354] She is assumed into heaven because it is not fitting that the corruption of death should touch her body. One of the oldest descriptions of this mystery comes from St. John Damascene.

> In the Holy and divinely-inspired Scripture no mention is made of anything concerning the end of Mary, the most holy Mother of God, but we have received from ancient and most truthful tradition that at the time of her glorious repose, all the Holy Apostles, who then were dispersed abroad in the world for the salvation of the nations, were in but a moment of time transported through the air to Jerusalem; and when they were there an angelic vision appeared to them and the divine chanting of the supernal powers were heard. And thus in divine and heavenly glory her holy soul was delivered in a way that no word can describe into the hands of God. And her body, which had been the Tabernacle of God after the chanting of the angels and the Apostles was finished and last respects were paid, was placed in a coffin in Gethsemani. [...]
>
> The Apostles were present there when Thomas, the only one who was absent, arrived after the third day, and since he wanted to worship the body that had been the Tabernacle of God they opened the coffin. And they were unable anywhere to find her most lauded body. [...] He (Christ) was pleased even after her departure from life to honor her immaculate and undefiled body with incorruption and with translation prior to the common and universal resurrection.[355]

In Mary's assumed body, the Church can experience the final consummation of the earthly pilgrimage and see a personal expression of the communion of the society of the Church at war with the dragon in the woman of the Apocalypse. She is "clothed with the sun, with the moon under her feet, and on her head a crown of twelve stars" (Rev. 12:1) because all nature finds it completion in man, and man finds his completion in God. The woman with her child struggle with the dragon as the woman and her child in Genesis 3:15 struggle with the serpent. These two experiences enclose the realization of salvation history in the rest of the Scripture like bookends. The pilgrim Church, struggling here on earth in faith, could not have a more powerful sign and advocate encouraging her members than Mary.

The veneration of Mary is founded on these mysteries and reflects the text of Scripture itself, "All generations will call me blessed." (Luke 1:48) The Church wants to be clear, again from an ecumenical intention, that the cultic veneration of Mary "for all its uniqueness, differs essentially from the cult of adoration, which is offered equally to the Incarnate Word and to the Father and the Holy Spirit and it is most favorable to it."[356] Marian piety must shun extremes which do not conform to the doctrine explained in Church teaching and be firmly rooted in the faith handed on through the Church. The veneration of Mary, called *hyperdulia* in Greek, and distinguished from the *latria* offered to God and the *dulia* offered to the rest of the saints, is based solidly on the Fathers and the Scholastic theologians. The Second Vatican Council points out, "[T]rue devotion consists neither in sterile nor transitory affection, nor in a certain vain credulity, but proceeds from true faith, by which we are to recognize the excellence of the Mother of God [...] and to the imitation of her virtues."[357]

Though the pious practices invoked as a result of private revelations are good when dogmatically based, Marian piety must be firmly based on public revelation and rooted in the liturgical expression of it approved by the hierarchy of the Church. If a private revelation teaches something contrary to the doctrine approved by the bishops and the Pope, it cannot be true. The communion in the Trinity of the Church as a society demands that Christ's Mother, who married the Trinity, cannot contradict Christ's Vicar, the Pope, as the representative of the hierarchial Church who has been given a special charism of the Holy Spirit to speak in its name.

Mary has a special cult of veneration in the Church expressed in divine worship, but this is of someone who cooperated with grace in the highest sense, not someone who gives these graces. Only God is the efficient cause of grace. Only Christ can merit grace by strict equality. Still, by the union of friendship, which unites God to man, it is a fittingly friendly thing that by proportional merit, through the communion of love, since man does God's will, "God should fulfill man's will in the salvation of another, although sometimes there can be an impediment on the part of the one whose justification the holy person desires."[358] This is a response by God to a proportional merit in the individual who, through the communion of love, does God's will.

There is no one more in love with God than Mary, and so, by the union of friendship, she is especially helpful in God doing man's will for our salvation. Her special cult in no way rivals the worship due to God and Christ alone, but supports it because no human being has ever worshipped God or loved Christ as much as the Savior's mother. She is not a priest as she does not offer the sacraments. Instead, she is the highest of believers as she benefits the most from all the actions of Christ, for she cooperates most through having a most prepared will.

The Church most fittingly ends her self-reflection on herself as the mysterious society on earth which has an earthly aspect but is in essence a communion with the Trinity, with a prayer for unity through the intercession of the Mother of God. Catholics and Orthodox likewise venerate her and see in her the sign of hope of the fullness of humanity which the divine light can bring. The faithful on earth experience in her one who lived faith, hope and charity to the fullness and now is enjoying the highest place in heaven. In the experience of the revelation of the "Light of the Nations" in the Church, she is truly "our life, our sweetness and our hope."[359]

Endnotes

[1] Karol Wojtyla, *Sources of Renewal* (San Francisco: Harper and Row, 1979), 36.

[2] Wojtyla, 35.

[3] Wojtyla, 35-36.

[4] The other is *Dei Verbum* on divine revelation.

[5] Joseph Cardinal Ratzinger, *The Ratzinger Report* (San Francisco: Ignatius, 1986), 41-42.

[6] Ratzinger, *Report*, 34-35.

[7] Henri de Lubac, *A Brief Catechesis of Nature and Grace* (San Francisco: Ignatius, 1984), 235-236.

[8] Ibid.

[9] Vatican II, *Synopsis Historica* (Bologna: Istituto per le Scienze Religiose, 1975).

[10] *The Gift of Infallibility*. Translated by James T. O'Connor (Boston: St. Paul Editions, 1986).

[11] John Paul II, *Address to the Conference Studying the Implementation of the Second Vatican Council*, February 27, 2000, n. 7.

[12] *Lumen Gentium*, chapter 7.

[13] "ad structuram constitutivam Ecclesiae" *Synopsis*, 483.

[14] "quasi monopolium" *Ibid.*

[15] "locum specialem" *Synopsis*, 482.

[16] "non est accidentalis" *Ibid.*

[17] "divina origo et intima natura" *Synopsis*, 484.

[18] *Ibid.*

[19] "...qui una cum Capite suo Summo Pontifice Corpus seu ordinem constituunt ..." *Ibid.*

[20] " ... in christiana obedientia et fiduciosa concordia ..." *Ibid.*

[21] *Ibid.*

[22] "... eius aestimatio inculcatur et foecunda operositas ostenditur ..." *Ibid.*

[23] *Ibid.*

[24] "Duplex est rei perfectio: prima et secunda. Prima quidem perfectio est, secundum quod res in sua substantia est perfecta. Quae quidem perfectio

est forma totius, quae ex integritate partium consurgit. Perfectio autem secunda est finis. Finis autem vel est operatio… vel est aliquid ad quod per operationem pervenitur… Prima autem perfectio est causa secundae: quia forma est principium operationis." Thomas Aquinas, *Summa Theologiae* (henceforth ST) I, 73, 1 ad corp. Cf. Also Aquinas, *De Veritate*, 1, 1, ad 9; ST, I, 48, 5, ad corp.; 111, 2, ad corp.; In Commentaria Super Sententias (SS) II, d. 35, 1, ad corp.; De Malo, 1, 4, 5, ad corp.; 16, 6, ad 4.

[25] "The Dogmatic Constitution *Lumen Gentium* was a true hymn of praise to the beauty of Christ's Bride." John Paul II, *Implementation of Vatican II*, n. 7.

[26] "Vox 'mysterium' non simpliciter indicat aliquid incognoscibile aut abstrusum, sed, uti hodie iam apud plurimos agnoscitur, designat realitatem divinam transcendentem et salvificam, quae aliquo modo visibili revelatur et manifestatur." *Synopsis*, 436.

[27] "Ecclesia ergo invisibilem continet et communicat gratiam quam ipsa significat. Hoc sensu analogico, ipsa appelatur 'sacramentum.'" *Catechism of the Catholic Church* (henceforth CCC) n. 774.

[28] "Ecclesia est simul: 'societas […] organis hierarchicis instructa et mysticum Christi corpus; coetus adspectabilis et communitas spiritualis; Ecclesia terrestris et Ecclesia caelestibus bonis ditata.' Hae dimensiones simul 'unam realitatem complexam efformant, quae humano et divino coalescit elemento.'" *CCC* n. 771.

[29] John Paul II, "Address to the Bishops of the United States of America," September 16, 1987, 1: *Insegnamenti di Giovanni Paolo II*, X, 3 (1987), 553; quoted in Congregation of the Doctrine of the Faith, "Some Aspects of the Church understood as Communion," n. 1.

[30] "[Alio modo] adiuvatur homo ex gratuita Dei voluntate, secundum quod aliquod habituale donum a Deo animae infunditur… Et sic donum gratiae qualitas quaedam est." Thomas Aquinas, ST, I-II, 110, 2, ad corp.

[31] "[…] autem Ecclesia sit in Christo veluti sacramentum seu signum et instrumentum intimae cum Deo unionis et totiusque generis humani unitatis," *Lumen Gentium* (henceforth LG), n. 1.

[32] Thomas Aquinas, *Summa Theologiae*, I, 43, 2, ad 3.

[33] "Mittens autem auctoritatem aliquam habet in missum. Oportet igitur dicere quod Filius habeat aliquam auctoritatem respectu Spiritus Sancti. Non autem dominii vel maioritatis, sed secundum solam originem." Thomas Aquinas, *Summa Contra Gentiles* (henceforth SCG), IV, 24, n. 3607.

34 "Sicut filius dicitur esse missus in mundum, inquantum novo modo per aliquem novum effectum incipit esse in mundo per visibilem carnem quam assumpsit ... dicitur etiam mitti spiritualiter et invisibiliter ad aliquem, inquantum per sapientiae donum in eo incipit inhabitare." Thomas Aquinas, *Contra Errores Graecorum*, 1, c, 14.

35 "Sic autem et Spiritus Sanctus visibiliter apparuit: vel in specie columbae super Christum in baptismo; vel in linguis igneis super Apostolos. Et licet no fuerit factus columba vel ignis, sicut Filius factus est homo tamen sicut in signis quibusdam ipsius in huiusmodi visibilibus speciebus apparuit; et sic etiam ipse quodam novo modo, scilicet, visibiliter, in mundo fuit." Thomas Aquinas, SCG, IV 23, n. 3594.

36 LG, 2.

37 "Sanguis et aqua quae de aperto Iesu crucifixi exiverunt latere, typi sunt Baptismi et Eucharistiae, vitae novae sacramentorum." CCC 1225.

38 "Sicut in ipsa persona Christi humanitas causat salutem nostram per gratiam, virtute divina principaliter operante; ita etiam in sacramentis novae legis, quae derivantur a Christo, causatur gratia instrumentaliter quidem per ipsa sacramenta, sed principalilter per virtutem Spiritus Sancti in sacramentis operantis." ST, I-II, 112, 1, ad 2.

39 "Sic appareat universa Ecclesia sicuti 'de unitate Patris et Filii et Spiritus Sancti plebs adunata.'" LG, 4, Cf. S. Cyprian, *De Oratione Domini*, 23: PL 4, 553.

40 Congregation for the Doctrine of the Faith, "Some Aspects of the Church Understood as Communion," May 28, 1992, n. 3.

41 "Plurimi Patres hoc thema exponi postulaverunt, quia abundanter in Evangeliis occurrit, et quia manifestat indolem simul visibilem et spiritualem societatis Ecclesiae, necnon aspectum eius historicum et eschatologicum." *Synopsis*, 438.

42 "Ecclesiae 'proprium est esse humanam simul ac divinam, visibilem invisibilibus praeditam, actione feventem et contemplationi vacantem, in mundo praesentem et tamen peregrinam: et ita quidem ut in ea quod humanum est ordinetur ad divinum eique subordinetur, quod visibile ad invisibile, quod actionis ad contempationem, et quod praesens ad futuram civitatem quam inquirimus." Vatican II, *Sacrosantum Concilium* (henceforth SC), 2, AAS 56 (1964) 98. Quoted in CCC 771.

43 "[...] exhibetur institutio Regni, tum praesertim in eius persona." *Synopsis*, 438.

44 "[...] Christum Dominium et regem misisse Spiritum Sanctum ad Ecclesiam, quae in terris inchoative Regnum Eius consitutit et quae ad gloriam finalem adspirat et perducit, [...]" *Ibid.*

45 "[...] Initium sumitur ab initiativa Dei, quae praesertim apparet in imaginibus a Pastore et ovibus desumptis." *Ibid.*

46 "Figurae ex agricultura et vinea depromptae speciatim descibunt semen Ecclesiae continuo crescens." *Ibid.*

47 "Imagines de aedificatione indicant progressivam et firmam exstructionem Ecclesiae." *Ibid.*

48 "Denique per figuram Sponsae insistitur super intimam unionem Christi et Ecclesiae, quae tamen a Sponso suo remanet distincta, eique fideliter oboediens." *Ibid.*

49 Wojtyla, *Sources*, 90-91.

50 "[...] inter thema de solidaritate omnium membrorum, quae per sacramenta in Corpore uniuntur, et thema de Capite Christo, qui super omnes eminet et corpus suum Spiritu suo donisque suis replet et crescere facit usque ad plenitudinem." *Synposis*, 438.

51 "[...] de corporibus nostris, quae per sacramenta sanctificantur, quia sacramenta etiam animam attingunt [...]." *Ibid.*

52 Ephesians 5: 21-23; 30.

53 "[...] Ecclesiam, cuius descripta est intima et arcana natura, qua cum Christo Eiusque opere in perpetuum unitur, his in terris concrete inveniri in Ecclesia catholica. Haec autem Ecclesia empirica mysterium revelat, sed non sine umbris, donec ad plenun lumen adducatur, sicut etiam Christus Dominus per exinanitionem ad gloriam pervenit." *Synopsis*, 439.

54 "Coetus autem visibilis et elementum spirituale non sunt duae res, sed una realitas complexa [...]." *Ibid.*

55 "[...] etiam in conditione paupertatis ac persecutiones, peccati et purificationis [...]." *Ibid.*

56 "Haec Ecclesia, in hoc mundo ut societas constituta et ordinata, subsistit in ecclesia catholica, a succesore Petri et Episcopis in eius communione gubernata [...]." LG, n. 8.

57 *Dominus Jesus* (henceforth DJ), Congregation for the Doctrine of the Faith, August 6, 2000.

58 DJ, n. 4.

59 "Quaedam verba mutantur: loco "est," l. 21, dicitur "subsistit in," ut expressio melius concordet cum affirmatione de elementis ecclesialibus quae alibi adsunt." *Synopsis*, 440.

60 DJ, n. 16.

61 *Ibid.*, quoting Vatican II, *Unitatis Redintegratio*, 3.

62 Hebrews 11:6.

63 Bede Jarrett, O.P., *Classic Catholic Meditations* (Manchester, New Hampshire: Sophia Institute Press, 2004), 246. (Originally published as *Meditations for Layfolk* (London: The Catholic Truth Society, 1941).

64 Charles Journet, *The Church of the Incarnate Word*, v. 1. Translated by A.H.C. Downes (New York: Sheed and Ward, 1955), 38.

65 "[...] ubi celebratio plene communio est et festum.' CCC, n.1136

66 "'Populus Dei' hic non intelligitur de grege fidelium, prout ab Hierarchia contradistinguitur, sed de toto complexu omnium, sive Pastorum sive fidelium, qui ad Ecclesiam pertinent." *Synopsis*, 441.

67 "Si verum est quod Hierarchia sub certo aspectu praecedit fideles, quos ad fidem et vitam supernaturalem generat, remanet tamen quod et Pastores et fideles ad unum pertinent Populum. Ipse Populus eiusque salus est in consilio Dei de ordine finis, dum Hierarchia ut medium ad hunc finem ordinatur. Populus imprimis in sua totalitate considerari fidelium, qui, conscii de sua personali responsabilitate, cum Pastoribus collaborare debent ad diffusionem ut ulteriorem sanctificationem totius Ecclesiae." *Ibid.*

68 "[...]sicut praecepta legis humanae ordinant hominem ad communitatem humanam, ita praecepta legis divinae ordinant hominem ad communitatem seu rempublicam hominum sub Deo." Thomas Aquinas, ST, I-II, 100, 5, ad corp.

69 "[...] inseparabile unitatis sacramentum [...]." LG, 9; see St. Cyprian, *Epist.*, 69, 6:PL 3.

70 "[...] licet essentia et non gradu tantum different [...]." LG, 10.

71 "[...] ad invicem ordinantur [...]." *Ibid.*

72 "tot ac tantis salutaribus mediis muniti, christifideles omnes, cuiusvis conditionis ac status ad perfectionem sanctitatis qua Pater ipse perfectus est, sua quisque via, a Domino vocantur." LG, 11.

73 [...] populus Dei sub ductu sacri magisterii, cui fideliter obsequens, iam non verbum hominum, sed vere accepit verbum Dei [...]." LG, 12.

74 *Ibid.*

75 "Agitur enim hic de toto Populo Dei, inclusa Hierarchia." *Synopsis*, 444.

76 "1)Maximi theologi post-Tridentini (M. Cano, S. Rob. Bellarmino, Gregorius de Valencia, Suarez, Gonet, Billuart) claret infallibilitatem fidelium in credenda docent. 2) Modus progrediendi eorum in expositione et argumentatione saepe explicite est 'a fidelibus ad hierarchiam,' seu ab

infallibilitate in credendo ad infallibilitatem in docendo; neque ullum in hoc vident periculum pro hierarchia. 3) Nequidem periculum vident in asserendo etiam a Romano Pontifice rationem esse habendam consensus fidelium." *Ibid.*

[77] "sacramenta et ministeria." LG 12.

[78] "temere expendenda." *Ibid.*

[79] It is strange that after the Council there was a great increase in Marian apparitions in which the visionaries sometimes claimed that the local bishop had no credibility in interpreting their truth. Such a claim is against the traditional teaching of the Church and also clearly contrary to the teaching of Vatican II.

[80] "Haec tamen Ecclesia una, inde ab origine sua, se cum magna praesentat diversitate, quae simul procedit e varietate donorum Dei et e multiplicitate personarum quae illa recipiunt. In populi Dei unitate diversitates congregantur populorum et culturarum." CCC n. 814.

[81] "simul transcendens et immanens." LG, 13.

[82] 'purificat, roborat et elevat." *Ibid.*

[83] "quae universo caritatis coetui praesidet." *Ibid.*

[84] "Haec est differentia inter corpus hominis naturale et corpus mysticum, quod membra corporis naturalis sunt omnia simul, membra autem corporis mystici non sunt omnia simul; neque quantum ad esse naturae, quia corpus Ecclesiae constituitur ex hominibus qui fuerunt a principio mundi usque ad finem ipsius; neque etiam quantum ad esse gratiae, quia eorum etiam qui sunt in uno tempore, quidam gratiae carent postmodum habituri, aliis eam iam habentibus. Sic igitur membra corporis mystici non solum accipiuntur secundum quod sunt in actu, sed etiam secundum quod sunt in potentia. [...] Sic ergo dicendum est quod, accipiendo generaliter secundum totum tempus mundi, Christus est caput omnium hominum: sed secundum diversos gradus. Primo enim et principaliter est caput eorum qui actu uniuntur sibi per gloriam. Secundo, eorum qui actu uniuntur sibi per caritatem. Tertio, eorum qui actu uniuntur sibi per fidem. Quarto vero eorum qui sibi uniuntur solum potentia [...]" Thomas Aquinas, ST, III, 8, 3, ad corp.

[85] "Ex alia parte catholici non 'coniunguntur' cum Ecclesia, sed ei 'incorporantur.'" *Synopsis*, 446.

[86] "Ecclesiam hanc peregrinantem necessariam esse ad salutem." LG, 14.

[87] "[...] illi homines salvari non possent [...] vel in eam intrare vel in eadem perservare noluerint." *Ibid.*

[88] "qui Spiritum Christi habentes." *Ibid.*

89 "professionis fidei, sacramentorum et ecclesiastici regiminis ac communionis." *Ibid.*

90 *Synopsis*, 446.

91 "Commissio admisit expressionem 'plene,' et delevit 'tantum,' ne excludantur pueri, usum rationis nondum habentes, vel etiam christiani rudiores, qui omnes conditiones implere et agnoscere non valent." *Ibid.*

92 Pius XII, *Mystici Corporis*, 1943.

93 "hoc ipso voto" LG, 14.

94 "explicita voluntate," *Ibid.*

95 'Sed Ecclesiae peregrinantis unitas etiam per visiblia communionis fulcitur vincula:—per unius fidei Professionem ab Apostolis receptae;—per communem cultus divini celebrationem, praesertim sacramentorum;—per apostolicam ope sacramenti Ordinis successionem, quae concordiam familiae Dei sustinet fraternam." CCC 815.

96 "Plene in communione Ecclesiae catholicae his in terris sunt illi baptizati, qui in eius compage visibili cum Christo coniunguntur, vinculis nempe professionis fidei, sacramentorum et ecclesiastici regiminis." *Code of Canon Law*, January 25, 1983, Canon 205.

97 Cf. John XXIII, *Ad Petri Cathedram*, where the Pope speaks of those who do not profess "either faith or communion with the Chair of Blessed Peter (*fidem vel communionem in Beati Petri Cathedra*)." Quoted in *Synopsis*, 447.

98 "communitatibus ecclesiasticis." LG, 15.

99 *Dominus Jesus*, n. 17.

100 LG, 15.

101 "episcopatu guadent, Sacram Eucharistiam celebrant necnon pietatem erga Deiparam Virginem fovent." *Ibid.*

102 "Documenta pontificia passim de 'Ecclesiis' orientalibus separatis loquuntur. Pro Protestantibus ultimi Pontifices adhibent vocem 'communitates christianae.'" Synopsis, 447.

103 "vera quaedam coniunctio." *Synopsis*, 447.

104 *Dominus Jesus*, 17 quoting John Paul II, Encyclical Letter *Ut unum sint*, 14 and Vatican II Decree *Unitatis Redintegratio*, 3 respectively.

105 "'Vera quaedam coniunctio.' Plures vellent supprimere vocem 'quaedam.' Hic enim indigitatur gratia sanctificans, quam Spiritus Sanctus virtute sua in christianis non-catholicis bene dispositis producit; 'quaedam' autem videtur induere sensum minus placentem. Commissio ideo addidit vocabulum 'vera,' ut vitetur interpretatio peiorativa; servavit tamen 'quaedam,'

ut ostendatur coniunctionem hanc inter Protestantes et Catholicos non esse perfectam." *Synopsis*, 447.

[106] "Ii tandem qui Evangelium nondum acceperunt ad Populum Dei diversis rationibus ordinantur." LG, 16.

[107] "Illi qui sunt infideles, etsi actu non sint de Eccelsia, sunt tamen in potentia. Quae quidem potentia in duobus fundatur: primo quidem et principaliter, in virtute Christi, quae sufficient est ad salutem totius humani generis; secondario, in arbitrii libertate." Thomas Aquinas, ST, III, 8, 3, ad 1.

[108] "Tamen possible est quod secundum diverse temporalium distinctio et explicatio ante Christi addendum revert, 'at quanta adventus Salvatoris vaccinatores existerent, tanto sacramenta salutis plenius preceperint.'" Thomas Aquinas, *Super Sententiarum III*, d. 25, 2, 2, qla. 3, ad corp.

[109] For a good summary of the ecclesiology of Rahner and especially his ideas about the "anonymous Christian," cf., for example, "Thus, even before Vatican II addressed itself to the prospects of salvation for those outside the Church, Rahner was promoting the belief both in the explicit offer of grace in the church, and in the 'anonymous' offer outside it," see Richard Lennan, *The Ecclesiology of Karl Rahner* (Oxford: Clarendon Press, 1995), 38. It is interesting that in the traditional doctrine, those who believe implicitly are members of the Church but just not full members.

[110] "Qui enim Evangelium christi Eiusque Ecclesiam sine culpa ignorantes, deum tamen sincero corde quaerunt, Eiusque voluntatem per conscientiae dictamen agnitam, operibus adimplere, sub gratiae influxu, conantur aeternam salutem consequi possunt. Nec divina Providentia auxilia ad salutem necessaria denegat his qui sine culpa ad expressam agnitionem Dei nondum pervenerunt et rectam vitam non sine divina gratia assequi nituntur." LG, 16.

[111] John Paul II, *Crossing the Threshold of Hope* (New York: Alfred A. Knopf, 1994), 77-104.

[112] *Crossing*, 81.

[113] *Crossing*, 89.

[114] *Crossing*, 92.

[115] *Crossing*, 99.

[116] "'[...] secundum antiquos Patres, quaenam elementa religiosa Evangelio prae-existere possint et tamquam praeparatio divinitus data considerari. Sunt autem semina veritatis, scilicet notiones de Deo et de anima aliaeque 'rationes universales.' De quibus agunt v.g. S. Iustinus, Tertullianus, Origenes." *Synposis*, 448.

[117] "sanetur, elevetur, et consummetur." LG, n. 17.

[118] John Paul II, *John Paul II in America* (Boston: St. Paul Books and Media, 1987) 192. Cited in Congregation of the Doctrine of the Faith, "Some Aspects of the Church Understood as Communion," n. 9.

[119] *Communion*, 9.

[120] John Paul II, *Sources of Renewal*, 147.

[121] "Quam doctrinam de institutione, perpetuitate, vi ac ratione sacri Primatus Romani Pontificis deque eius infallibili Magisterio, Sacra Synodus cunctis fidelibus firmiter credendam rursus proponit [...]," LG, 18.

[122] "Christus Dominius [...] in Ecclesia sua varia ministeria instituit, quae ad bonum totius Corporis tendunt." *Ibid.*

[123] "[...] qui sacra potestate pollent [...]," *Ibid.*

[124] "[...] beatum Petrum ceteris Apostolis praeposuit in ipsoque instituit perpetuum ac visible unitatis fidei et communionis principium et fundamentum." *Ibid.* Cf. Vatican Council I, Session, IB, Const. Dogm. *Pastor Aeternus*: D-S 1821 (3050 f.).

[125] "[...] et in eodem incepto pergens, doctrinam de Episcopis, successoribus Apostolorum, qui cum successore Petri, Christi Vicario ac totius Ecclesiae visibili Capite, domum Dei viventis regunt, coram omnibus profiteri et declarare constituit." LG, 18.

[126] John Paul II, *John Paul II in America*, 1.

[127] Extraordinary Session of the Synod of Bishops, *Relatio Finalis*, c. 1, 1985.

[128] *Some Aspects*, 3.

[129] *Some Aspects*, 4.

[130] *Some Aspects*, 9. Cf. John Paul II, "Address to the Roman Curia," December 20, 1990, 9: AAS 83 (1991), 745-747.

[131] [Q]uos Apostolos (cf. Lc. 6, 13) ad modum collegii seu coetus stablilis instituit, cui ex eiisdem electum Petrum praefecit [...]." LG, 19.

[132] "Vocabulum collegium non sensu iuridico de coetu perfectae aequalium intelligitur; sed de coetu starili, a Domino instituto." *Synopsis*, 450.

[133] "Collegium non intelligitur sensu stricte iuridico, scilicet de coetu aequalium, qui potestatem suam praesidi suo demandarent, sed de coetu stabili, cuius structura et auctoritas ex Revelatione deduci debent." LG, *Nota explicita praevia*, 1.

[134] "Aliis verbis distinctio non est inter Romanum Pontificem et Episcopos collective sumptos, sed inter Romanum Pontificem simul cum Episcopis." *Nota praevia*, 3.

[135] "Factum talis successionis etiam patet ex testimonio S. Clementis Rom. 44, 3. In genere autem indicationes scripturisticae in Traditione clarificantur." *Synopsis*, 451.

[136] "[...] doctrinam, cultum et regimen [...]." *Synopsis*, 452.

[137] "Similiter Commissio non expresse intrat, ut voluerunt tamen E/961 aliique, in distinctionem inter praerogativas personales, quas Duodecim, utpote fundatores Ecclesiae, transmittere non debebant, et munera successoribus continuanda. Dicit tamen explicite quod permanet munus Apostolorum pascendi Ecclesiam." *Ibid.*

[138] LG, 21.

[139] "actio Christi," *Synopsis*, 452.

[140] "[...] et ipsis audiutoribus suis per impositionem manuum donum spirituale tradiderunt (cf. 1 Tim. 4, 14; 2 Tim 1, 6-7), quod usque ad nos in episcopali consecratione transmissum est. Docet autem Sancta Synodus episcopali consecratione plenitudinem conferri sacramenti Ordinis ..." LG, 21.

[141] "Membrum Corporis episcopalis aliquis constituitur vi sacramentalis consecrationis et hierarchia communione cum Collegii Capite atque membris." LG 22.

[142] In consecratione datur ontologica participatio sacrorum munerum ..." *Nota Praevia*, 2.

[143] "[...] ita conferri et sacrum characterem ita imprimi, ut Episcopi, eminenti ac adspectabili modo, ipsius Christi Magistri, Pastoris, et Pontificis partes sustineant et in Eius persona agant." LG, 21.

[144] John Paul II, Address to the U.S. Catholic Bishops, Los Angeles, September 16, 1987, nn. 3 and 4 in *John Paul II in America*, 193.

[145] "Ex desiderio autem S. Pontificis petitum est a Pont. Commissione Biblica, utrum [...] S. Petrum et ceteros Apostolos unum collegium apostolicum constituere. Responsum Commissionis Biblicae est positivum." *Synopsis*, 454.

[146] "Singuli Episcopi, qui particularibus Ecclesiis praeficiuntur, regimen summ pastorale super portionem Populi Dei sibi commissam, non super alias Ecclesias neque super Eccleiam universalem exercent." LG, 23.

[147] "[...] plenam, supremam, et universalem, potestatem, quam semper libere exercere valet." LG, 22.

[148] "Concilium Oecumenicum numquam datur, quod a Successore Petri non sit ut tale confirmatum vel saltem receptum." *Ibid.*

[149] "supremae ac plenae potestatis." *Ibid.*

[150] "[..] una cum Capite suo Romano Pontifice, et numquam sine hoc Capite, subiectum quoque supremae ac plenae potestatis in universum Ecclesiam exsistit." *Ibid.*

[151] "Collegium autem seu corpus Episcoporum auctoritatem non habet, nisi simul cum Pontifice Romano, successore Petri, ut capite eius intellegatur [. . .]." *Ibid.*

[152] LG, 23.

[153] John Paul II, Apostolic Letter *Apostolos Suos* (On the Theological and Juridical Nature of Episcopal Conferences,) May 21, 1998, 14. Cf. Code of Canon Law, Canon 447; Second Vatican Ecumenical Council, Decree on the Pastoral Office of Bishops in the Church, *Christus Dominius*, 37.

[154] *Apostolos Suos*, 12.

[155] John Paul II, Speech to the Bishops of the United States of America (September 16, 1987), 3. Quoted in *Apostolos Suos*, 12.

[156] *Apostolos*, 20.

[157] *Apostolos*, 22.

[158] Vincent Gasser, *The Gift of Infallibility*. Translated with commentary by James T. O'Connor (Boston: St. Paul Editions, 1986), 23, translator's commentary.

[159] "Gasser, Vinzenz Ferrer," *The New Catholic Encyclopedia*, vol. VI (Washington: McGraw-Hill Book Company, 1967), 299.

[160] For the examination of the teaching of Bishop Gasser in the following pages, I am indebted to Fr. Ulrich Hörst, O.P. and his class notes for the class "Papal Infallibility" taught at the Angelicum University circa 1981. I will cite these as Hörst.

[161] "Infallibilitas absoluta competit soli Deo [. . .] Omnis alia infallibilitas utpote communicata ad certum finem habet suos limites et suas conditiones [. . .]." Gasser, *Mansi*, 52, 1214 AB.

[162] Hörst, *Notes*, 19.

[163] Gasser-O'Connor, *Mansi* 1216, Gift, 50.

[164] Gasser-O'Connor, *Mansi* 1225, Gift, 73.

[165] Hörst, *Notes*, 23.

[166] Cf. Gasser-O'Connor, *Mansi* 1223, Gift, 66-67.

[167] Gasser-O'Connor, *Mansi* 1215, Gift, 47.

[168] "Eadem infallilbilitas agnoscitur quoque Corpori Episcoporum, quando simul cum Romano Pontifice definitionem profert. Quod ad objectum praecipuum et directum huius paragraphi pertinet." *Synopsis*, 459.

[169] *Synopsis*, 458.

[170] "Infallibilitas qua Christus Ecclesiam instructam esse voluit prorsus identificatur cum infallibilitate Ecclesiae docentis; et quidem: sive totius Episcopatus, sive singulariter Romani Pontificis." *Ibid.*

[171] "Qua quidem infallibilitate Romanus Pontifex, Collegii Episcoporum Caput, vi muneris sui gaudet, quando ut supremus omnium christifidelium pastor et doctor, qui fratres suos in fide confirmat, doctrinam de fide vel moribus definitivo actu proclamat." LG, 25.

[172] "Infallibilitas Ecclesiae promissa in corpore Episcoporum quoque inest, quando supremum magiterium cum Petri successore exercet." *Ibid.*

[173] Josef Cardinal Ratzinger, *Doctrinal Commentary of the Concluding Formula of the Professio Fidei,* Congregation for the Doctrine of the Faith, June 29, 1998, 5.

[174] *Professio,* 11.

[175] *Professio,* 5.

[176] "Infallibilitas qua Christus Ecclesiam instructam esse voluit prorsus identificatur cum infallibilitate Ecclesiae docentis; et quidem: sive totius Episcopatus, sive singulariter Romani Pontificis." *Synopsis,* 458.

[177] *Professio,* 6.

[178] *Ibid.*

[179] *Ibid.*

[180] *Professio,* 11.

[181] *Ibid.*

[182] *Professio,* 9.

[183] "Licet singuli praesules infallibilitatis praerogativa non pollent, quando tamen, etiam per orbem dispersi, sed communionis nexum inter se et cum Successore Petri servantes, authentice res fidei et morum docentes in unam sententiam tamquam definitive tenendam conveniunt, doctrinam Christi infallibiliter enuntiant." LG, 25.

[184] *Professio,* 10.

[185] *Ibid.*

[186] *Professio,* 11. Cf. "This loyal submission of the will and intellect must be given in a special way to the authentic teaching of the Roman Pontiff, even when he does not speak *ex cathedra,* in such wise, indeed, that his supreme teaching authority be acknowledged with respect and sincere assent be given to decisions made by him, conformably with his manifest mind and intention, which is made known principally either by the character of the documents in question, or by the frequency with which a certain doctrine is proposed, or by the manner in which the doctrine is formulated." LG, 25.

187 "Eadem infallibilitas agnoscitur quoque Corpori Episcoporum, quando simul cum Romano Pontifice definitionem profert. Quod ad obiectum praecipuum et directum huius paragraphi pertinet." *Synopsis*, 459.

188 "Collegium, quod sine Capite non datur, dicitur: 'subiectum quoque supremae ac plenae potestatis in universam Ecclesiam existere.' [...] Aliis verbis distinctio non est inter Romanum Pontificem et Episcopos collective sumptos, sed inter Romanum Pontificem seorsim et Romanum Pontificem simul cum Episcopis. Quia vero Summus Pontifex est Caput Collegii, ipse solus quosdam actus facere potest, qui Episcopis nullo modo competunt [...] Ad iudicum Summi Pontificis, cui cura totius gregis Christi commissa est, spectat, secundum necessitates Ecclesiae decursu temporum variantes, determinare modum quo haec cura actuari conveniat, sive modo personali, sive modo collegiali. Romanus Pontifex ad collegiale exercitium ordinandum, promovendum, approbandum, intuitu boni Ecclesiae, secundum propriam discretionem procedit." Vatican II, *Nota Praevia* to *Lumen Gentium*, 3, 4.

189 "[...] sed consensus totius communitatis secum ferant et exprimant." *Synopsis*, 459.

190 *Code of Canon Law Annotated*, eds. E. Capparos, M. Theriault, J. Thorn, (Montreal: Wilson and LaFleur Limitee, 1992), 419.

191 "Consideratur autem Ecclesia particularis praesertim infra diocesim, sive sit paroecialis, sive alia ratione convocetur, semper tamen sub dependentia ab Episcopo." *Synopsis*, 459.

192 : [...] oratione, praedicatione, sacramentorum adminstratione et etiam exemplo."

193 "[...] obligatio perpetua ad ea quae sunt perfectionis, cum aliqua solemnitate." ST, II-II, 184, 5, ad corp.

194 Ibid., 7 ad corp.

195 "[...] mores suos ab omni malo temperantes et quantum poterint [...]" LG, 26.

196 Cf. *ARCC/ Vatican 2*. Site Editor: Ingrid H. Shafer, Ph.D.

197 "The Battle for the Keys," *Inside the Vatican*, June-July (2002): 26.

198 "Battle, 26.

199 "Giancarlo Zizola, who lives in Rome, is considered the dean of today's Vaticanologists. He has covered the Vatican for publications in many countries since before Vatican II. Many of his books, which include biographies of Popes John XXIII and Paul VI, have been widely translated." *National Catholic Reproter*, October 4, 2002.

200 *Ibid.*

[201] *Ibid.*, 28.

[202] " [...] vicarii et legati [...]," LG, 28.

[203] " [...] neque vicarii Romanorum Pontificum putandi sunt [...]," *Ibid.*

[204] " [...] propria, ordinaria et immediate [...]," *Ibid.*

[205] " [...] leges ferendi, iudicium faciendi et variis modis administrandi [...]," *Synopsis*, 460.

[206] " [...] sacrum ius et coram Domino officium [...]," LG, 27.

[207] "[...] licet a suprema Ecclesiae auctoritate exercitium eiusdem ultimatum regetur [...]," *ibid.*

[208] George Weigel, *The Courage to be Catholic* (New York, New York: Basic Books, 2002), 114.

[209] *Ibid.*, 200.

[210] *Ibid.*, 199.

[211] Pope John Paul II, *Apostolos Suos*, On the Theological and Juridical Nature of Episcopal Conferences, Rome, 1998, n. 14 (henceforth AS).

[212] AS, n. 18.

[213] AS, n. 12.

[214] Yves Congar, O.P., "The apostolic college, primacy and episcopal conferences, *"Theology Digest"* 34:3 (Fall 1987), 211.

[215] Francis A. Sullivan, S.J., *"The Teaching Authority of Episcopal Conferences,"* Theological Studies, 63 (2002), 485.

[216] *Ibid.*, 488.

[217] AS, n. 22.

[218] "Sic ministerium ecclesiasticum divinitus institutum diversis ordinibus exercetur ab illis qui iam ab antiquo Episcopi, Prebyteri, Diaconi vocantur." LG, n. 28.

[219] " [...] consecrantur [...]," *Ibid.*

[220] " [...] Episcopos [...] presbyteris tam ordine quam iurisdictione ex divina institutione superiores esse." Reformed schema for Vatican I, c. 4: Mansi 53, 310. Quoted in *Synopsis*, 461.

[221] " [...] ad Evangelium praedicandum fidelesque pascendos et ad divinum cultum celebrandum consecrantur, ut veri sacerdotes Novi Testamenti [...]," LG, 28.

[222] " [...] licet essentia et non gradu tantum different [...]," LG, n. 10.

[223] " [...] in persona Christi agentes [...] unicum sacrificium Novi Testamenti [...] repraesentant et applicant." LG, n. 28.

[224] Josef Pieper, "What is a Priest? An Urgent Effort at Clarification,"

Problems of Modern Faith, (Chicago: Franciscan Herald Press, 1985), 59-115.

[225] Pieper, "Priesthood," 62.

[226] "Et hoc utique sacramentum nemo potest conficere, nisi sacerdos, qui rite fuerit ordinatus, secundum claves Ecclesiae, quas ipse concessit Apostolis eorumque successoribus Iesus Christus." IV Lateran Council, c. 1; D. 802.

[227] "[...] quod actus aliqui immediate ad deum ordinantur dupliciter. Uno modo ex parte unius personae tantum, sicut facere singulares orationes, et vovere, et huiusmodi; et talis actus competit cuilibet baptizato. Alio modo ex parte totius ecclesiae; et sic solus sacerdos habet actus immediate ad deum ordinatos, quia ipse solus potest gerere actus totius ecclesiae qui consecrat eucharistiam quae sacramentum universalis ecclesiae." *Super Sententiarum*, IV, d. 24, 2, 2, ad 2.

[228] "[Contra Haec] in memoriam revocandum esse ducimus, sacerdotem nempe idcirco tantum populi vices agere, quia personam gerit Dni. N. Iesu Christi, quatenus membrorum omnium Caput est, pro iisdem semet ipsum offert." Pius XII, *Mediator Dei*. D. 3850.

[229] "Quare sacerdotium Presbyterorum initiationis christianae Sacramenta quidem supponit, peculiari tamen illo sacramento confertur, quo Presbyteri, unctione Spiritus Sanctus, speciali charactere signantur et sic Christo Sacerdoti configurantur, ita ut in persona Christ Capitis agere valeant." *Presbyterorum Ordinis*, n. 2.

[230] I am indebted for many of the ideas in this section to the excellent article already cited from Josef Pieper. Though I quote from this article my dependence on it involves ideas too many to be cited. The reader is urged to read this excellent article.

[231] Pieper, *Priesthood*, 66.

[232] *Ibid.*

[233] *Ibid.*, 67.

[234] For example, *Pastores Gregis*, n. 17; Augustine, *Sermo*, 340, 1: PL 38, 1483.

[235] " [...] potestate sacra [...]," LG, n. 10.

[236] " [...] sacrificium eucharisticum in persona Christi conficit illudque nomine totius populi Deo offert." LG, n. 10.

[237] SC, n. 10.

[238] "[...] in aliis sacramentis consecratio materiae consistit solum in quadam benedictione, ex qua materia consecrata accipit instrumentaliter quandam spirtualem virtutem quae per ministrum, qui est instrumentum animatum,

potest ad instrumenta inanimata producere. Sed in hoc sacramento consecratio materiae consistit in quadam miraculosa conversione substantiae,
quae a solo Deo perfici potest. Unde minister in hoc sacramento perfici-
endo non habet alium actum nisi prolationem verborum. [. . .] Sed forma
huius sacramenti profertur ex persona ipsius Christi loquentis; ut detur
intelligi quod minister in perfectione huius sacramenti nihil agit nisi quod
profert verba Christi." Aquinas, ST, III, 78, 1, ad corp.

[239] "[. . .] sacerdotes ad hoc consecrantur ut sacramentum Corporis Christi
conficiant [. . .]," ST, III, 67, 2, ad corp.

[240] "Cum enim nemo salvari posit, qui prius non crediderit, Presbyteri,
utpote Episcoporum cooperatores, primum habent officum Evangelium
Dei omnibus evangelizandi [. . .]." Vatican II, *Presbyterorum Ordinis*
(henceforth PO), n. 4.

[241] "Suum vero munus sacrum maxime exercent in eucharistico cultu vel
synaxi, qua in persona Christi agentes [. . .]." LG, n. 28.

[242] "Quapropter Eucharistia ut fons et culmen totius evangelizationis apparet." PO, n. 5.

[243] John M. Huerls, O.S.M., *The Pastoral Companion* (Quincy, IL: Franciscan
Press, 1995), 91. Reference in this quote is: "See CodCom, interpretation,
May 26, 1987, AAS 79 (1987) 1249; BCL Newsletter 24 (1988) 103."

[244] "Quapropter nemo omnino alius, etiamsi sit sacerdos, quidquam proprio
marte in Liturgia addat, demat, aut mutet." *Sacrosanctum Concilium*, n.
22 n. 3; CIC, Canon 846 n. 1; *Euchariticum Mysterium* n. 45; GIRM,
n. 24.

[245] "Functio rectorum communtatis ("presbyteri") cum functione cultica
("sacerdotes") coniuncta apparet." *Synopsis*, 461.

[246] "[. . .] unum altare, sicut unus episcopus cum presbyterio et diaconis [..],"
Ignatius of Antioch, *Letter to the Philadelphians*, 4; ed. Funk, I, 4.

[247] Presbyteri, ordinis Episcopalis providi cooperatores eiusque adiutorium
et organum, [. . .] unum presbyterium cum suo Episcopo constituunt,
diversis quidem officiis mancipatum." LG, n. 28.

[248] "[. . .] presbyteros autem ut senatum Dei et concilium apostolorum [. . .],"
Ignatius of Antioch, *Letter to the Trallians*, n. 3, 1.

[249] "[. . .] *sub auctoritate* (it. original) Episcopi et non propie nomine eius
[. . .]," *Synopsis*, 461-2.

[250] "*obediencia et fiducia*" [it. original], *Ibid.*

[251] "paternus et amicalis affectus," *Ibid.*

[252] CCC n. 306.

[253] Conrad Baars, "Psychological Aspects of Obedience," *Cross and Crown*,
XVII, nn. 1-3 (1965), 16.

254
In this section, I am greatly indebted to the very insightful ideas and expressions of Dr. Conrad Baars in his article, "The Psychological Aspects of Obedience," *Cross and Crown*, XVII, nn. 1-3 (1965) 1-37. The citations from this article are too many to be noted.

255
Thomas Aquinas, ST, II-II, 105, 1, ad 3.

256
"Vi communis sacrae ordinationis et missionis Presbyteri omnes inter se intima fraternitate nectuntur, quae sponte ac libenter sese manifestet in mutuo anxilio, tam spirituali quam materiali, tam pastorali quam personali, in conventibus et communione vitae, laboris et caritatis." LG, 28.

257
"[...] non ad sacerdotium, sed ad ministerium [...]," LG 29.

258
"[...] ad ministerium Episcopi [...]," *Synopsis*, 462.

259
"[...] in diakonia liturgiae, verbi et caritatis [...]," *Ibid.*

260
"Nomine laicorum hic intelligitur omnes chistifideles praeter membra ordinis sacri et status religiosi in Ecclesia sanciti [...]," LG, 31.

261
"Ponitur statui laicorum, loco condicioni et missioni (quae verba paulo post recurrunt), ut laicatui agnoscatur in Ecclesia honor constituendi statum, saltem sensu lato." *Synopsis*, 467.

262
"[...] programmaticus [...]." *Ibid.*

263
"[...] scriptum super portas Concilii [...]" from an allocution of John XIII for the day of Pentecost, 1960 quoted in *Synopsis*, 467.

264
Jordan Aumann, O.P., *On the Front Lines*, (New York: Alba House, 1990) 67.

265
"[...] indolis secularis [...]" *Synposis* 467.

266
Aumann, *Lines*, 68.

267
Quoted in Aumann *Lines* 68.

268
"Sicut dictum est, congruum erat incarnationis fini ut Christus non ageret solitariam vitam, sed cum hominibus conversaretur. Qui autem cum aliquibus conversatione conformet." ST, III, 40, 2, ad corp.

269
"[...] ita etiam fratres habent eos [...]," LG, 32.

270
"[...] contactus personales [...]," *Synopsis*, 468.

271
"[...] occasionalis et suppletiva [...]," *Ibid.*

272
"Distinguit Subcommissio sat clare inter apostolatum generalem et apostolatum strictioris sensus, scilicet ex mandato. [...] Communis ergo vocatio ad apostolatum distinguitur a formis specialibus sub 'magis immediata' responsibilitate Hierarchiae." *Ibid.*

273
"Praeterea aptitudine gaudent, ut ad quaedam munera ecclesiastica, ad finem spirtualem exercenda, ab Hierarchia adsumantur," LG 33.

274
"Vitatur tamen nimis rigida applicatio istius triplicis muneris, ne tripartitio theologiae imponatur." *Synopsis*, 469.

275 "Unde magis respicitur ad sensum, nempe ad cultum, ad testimonium et ad servitium in communione." *Ibid.*

276 "[...] Patri piissime offeruntur [...]," LG, 34.

277 "Sic et laici, qua adoratores ubique sancta agentes, ipsum mundum Deo consecrant." *Ibid.*

278 J.P. De Caussade, *The Abandonment to Divine Providence*, I, 1, 1.

279 "Notandum est hic, quod quatuor sacramenta dicuntur magna, scilicet Baptismus ratione effectus, quia delet culpam et aperit ianuam paradisi; Confirmatio ratione ministri, quia solum a pontificis et non ab aliis confertur; Eucharistia ratione continentiae, quia totum Christum continet; item Matrimonium ratione significationis, quia significat coniunctionem Christi et Ecclesiae." Thomas Aquinas, *Comm. ad Ephesios*, V, 1. 10, n. 334.

280 Thomas Aquinas, *De Malo*, 15, 2, corp.

281 John Paul II, *Familiaris Consortio*, 21; cf. LG 11.

282 Thomas Aquinas, Summa contra Gentiles, IV, 58; quoted in John Paul II, *Familiaris Consortio*, 38.

283 Francis de Sales, *Introduction to the Devout Life*, III, 1.

284 "Ad tertium dicendum quod multiplex est instructio. Una conversiva ad fidem. Quam dionysius attribuit episcopo, in II Cap. Eccl. Hier., et potest competere cuilibet praedicatori, vel etiam cuilibet fideli. Secunda est intructio qua quis eruditur de fidei rudimentis, et qualiter se debeat hebere in susceptione sacramentorum. Et haec pertinet secundario quidem ad ministros, principaliter autem ad sacerdotes. Tertia est instructio de conversatione christianae vitae. Et haec pertinet ad patrinos. Quarta est instructio de profundis mysteriis *findei*, et prefectione christianae vitae. Et haec ex officio pertinet ad episcopos." ST, III, 71, 4, ad 3.

285 "Reges sunt in eos non regant peccatum, qui dominantur corporis sui, [...] Hi ergo reges sunt, et horum Deus rex est." St. Hilary, *In Pslamis*, PL 9, 465 CSEL 135,6; col. 771 (Zingerle), p. 717.

286 *Synopsis*, 470.

287 "Propter ipsam oeconomiam salutis, fideles discant sedulo distinguere inter iura et officia quae eis imcumbunt, quatenus Ecclesiae aggregantur, et ea quae eis competent, ut sunt humanae societatis membra." LG, 36.

288 Pius XI, *Divini Redemptoris*, n. 29.

289 John Paul II, *The Acting Person*, 341.

290 John Paul II, *Acting*, 340.

291 "Sicut enim agnoscendum est terrnam civitatem, saecularibus curis iure addictam propriis regi principiis, ita infausta doctrina, quae societatem,

nulla habita religionis ratione, exstruere contendit et libertatem religiosam civium impugnat et eruit, mertio reiicitur." LG, 36.

[292] " [...] verbi Dei praesertim et sacramentorum adiumenta [...]," LG 37.

[293] "Laici, sicut omnes christifideles, illa quae sacri Pastores, utpote Christum repraesentantes, tamquam magistri et rectores in Ecclesia statuunt, christiana oboedientia prompte amplectantur [...], *Ibid.*

[294] "Uno verbo, 'quod anima est in corpore, hoc sint in mundo christiani," *Epistle to Diognetus*, 6: ed. Funk, I, p. 400; quoted in LG, 38.

[295] CCC, Section II, article 9, Paragraph 2, Title.

[296] "Ulterius post expositionem de 'constitutione hierarchia', Schema animum diserte vertit ad 'finem' ab Ecclesia intentum [...]." *Synopsis*, 484.

[297] "[...] indefectibiliter sancta [...]," LG, 39.

[298] "Christus qui "solus sanctus" est, etiam Ecclesiam quam fundavit, sanctam voluit et fecit." Synopsis, 472.

[299] "Additur finis ipsius sanctitatis: ad gloriam Dei." *Ibid.*

[300] "[...] in *suo aspectu ontologico* (it. original), *et in suo fine* (it. original)." *Synopsis*, 472.

[301] "Cunctis proinde perspicuum est, omnes christifideles cuiuscumque status vel ordinis ad viate christinae plenitudinem et caritatis perfectionem vocari, qua sanctitate, [...]," LG, 40.

[302] John Paul II, *Starting afresh from Christ*, n. 28.

[303] CCC, n. 2011.

[304] *Redemptionis Sacramentum*, n. 19; Vatican II, *Christus Dominus*, n. 15; *Sacrosanctum Concilium*, n. 41; Code of Canon Law, 387.

[305] Jordan Aumann and Conrad Baars, *The Unquiet Heart* (New York: Alba House, 1991) 156.

[306] *Redemptionis Sacramentum*, n. 44, cf. Pius XII, *Mediator Dei*: AAS 39 (1947) p. 553; John Paul II, *Ecclesia de Eucharistia*, n. 29.

[307] "Pro plebe sua et toto Poppulo Dei ex officio precantes et sacrificium offerentes, agnoscendo quod agunt et imitando quod tractant [...]," LG, 41.

[308] Code of Canon Law, 276, n. 2, paragraph 3.

[309] *The Code of Canon Law: A Text and Commentary*, eds. Coridan, Green, Heintshel (New York: Paulist Press, 1985) 207.

[310] Francis de Sales, *Introduction to the Devout Life*, III, 1.

[311] *Ibid.*

[312] Conrad W. Baars, *Doctor of the Heart* (New York: Alba House, 1996), 186.

[313] Aelred Squire, *Asking the Fathers* (Westminster. Maryland: Christian Classics, 1973), 41.

[314] "[…] abrenuntiatio propriarum facultatum dupliciter considerari potest. Uno modo, secundum quod est in actu. Et sic in ea non consistit essentialiter perfectio, sed est quoddam perfectionis instrumentum […] Et ideo nihil prohibit statum perfectionis esse sine abrenuntiatione propriorum. Sic dicendum aliis exterioribus observantiis. Alio modo potest considerari secundum praeparationem animi: ut scilicet homo sit paratus, si opus fuerit, omnia dimittere, vel distribuere." Thomas Aquinas, ST, II-II, 184, 7, ad 1.

[315] CCC, n. 2725.

[316] Sister Sandra Schneiders, *St. Louis Review*, Oct. 20, 1995, quoted in Ann Carey, *Sisters in Crisis* (Huntington, Indiana: Our Sunday Visitor, INC., 1997), p. 302.

[317] John Paul II, *Vita Consecrata*, (March 25, 1996), n. 32; cf. Council of Trent, Session XXIV, Canon 10; DS 1810; Piius XII, *Sacra Virginitas* (March 25, 1954): AAS 46 (1954), 176.

[318] CCC, n. 1973.

[319] "Consilia evangelica castitatis Deo dicatae, paupertatis, et oboedientiae, utpote in verbis et exemplis Dominini fundata et ab Apostolis et Patribus Ecclesiaeque doctoribus et pastoribus commendata, sunt donum divinum, quod Ecclesia a Domino accepit et gratia Eius semper conservat," LG, 43.

[320] "Status huiusmodi, ratione habita divinae et hierarchicae Ecclesiae constitutionis, non est intermedius inter clericalem et laicalem […]." *Ibid*.

[321] "Status ergo, qui professione consiliorum evangelicorum constituitur, licet ad Ecclesiae structuram hierarchicam non spectet, ad eius tamen vitam et sanctitatem inconcusse pertinet," LG, n. 44.

[322] "Si vero [aliquis] totam vitam suam voto Deo obligavit, ut in operibus prefectionis ei deserviat, iam simpliciter conditionem vel statum perfectionis assumpsit." Thomas Aquinas, *De Perfectione Vitae Spiritualis*, c. 15; quoted in *Synopsis*, 480.

[323] "[…] ut autem gratiae baptismalis uberiorem fructum percipere queat, consiliorum evangeliorum professione in Ecclesia liberari intendit ab impedimentis, quae ipsum a caritatis fervore et divini cultus perfectione retrahere possent et divino obequio intimius consecratur," LG, n. 44.

[324] John Paul II, *Vita Consecrata*, 51.

[325] John Paul II, *Novo Millennio Ineunte*, n. 43.

[326] *Preface for Virgins and Religious*.

[327] *Code of Canon Law*, Canon 590.

328 "Omnes tandem perspectum habeant, consiliorum evangelicorum professionem, quamvis renuntiationem secumferat bonorum quae indubie magni aesitmanda veniunt, tamen personae humanae vero profectui non obstare, sed natura sua ei summopere prodesse." LG, 46.

329 "Pius XII, Alloc. Annus sacer, 8 dec. 1950, l. c., p. 30, docet statum religiosum non esse salutis refugium timentibus et anxiis datum, sed magnum spiritum et se devovendi stadium flagitare [...]," *Synopsis*, 481.

330 "Consilia enim, secundum cuiusquam personalem vocationem voluntarie suscepta, ad cordis purificationem et spiritualem libertatem non parum conferunt, fervorem caritatis iugiter excitant [...]." LG, 46.

331 "Hoc caput introductum est secundum voluntatem S.P. Ioannis XXIII [...]," *Synopsis*, 485.

332 "De indole eschatological Ecclesiae peregrinantis eiusque unione cum Ecclesia coelesti." LG, Title of Chapter Seven.

333 "Ecclesia, ad quam in Christo Jesu vocamur omnes in qua per gratiam Dei sanctitatem acquirimus, nonnisi in Gloria coelesti consummabitur, quando adveniet tempus restitutionis omnium." LG, n. 48.

334 "[...] l ex vetus non solum fuit Patris, sed etiam Filii; quia Christus in veteri lege figurabatur. Unde Dominus dicit Ioan. 5:46: 'Si crederetis Moysi, crederetis forsitan et mihi: de me enim ille scripsit.' Similiter etiam lex nova non solum est Christi, sed etiam Spiritus Sancti; secundum illud Rom. 8:2: 'Lex Spiritus vitae in Christo Jesu, etc.' Unde non est expectanda alia lex, quae sit Spiritus Sancti." Thomas Aquinas, ST, I-II, 106, 4, ad 3.

335 CCC, n. 1139.

336 "[...] etenim Ecclesia iam in terris vera sanctitate licet imperfecta insignitur." LG, n. 48.

337 Francis de Sales, *Letters of Francis de Sales and Jane Frances de Chantal*, Paulist Press, 173.

338 Hugh Barbour, O. Praem., "Bonum Communius Ente" (Congresso Tomista Internazionale: Rome, Italy, 2003), 9.

339 "In numero 49 et in sequenti provisum est ut textus ostenderet ultimum fundamentum doctrinale totius Capitis, scilicet quod Ecclesia terrestris et coelestis unum Populum Dei et unum Iesu Christi Mysticum Corpus constituunt." *Synopsis*, n. 485.

340 "Omnes tamen, gradu quidem modoque diverso, in eadem Dei et proximi caritate communicamus et eundem hymnun gloriae Deo nostro canimus." LG, n. 49.

341 "[...] si loquamur de felicitate praesentis vitae, [...] felix indiget amicis, non quidem propter utilitatem, cum sit sibi sufficiens; nec propter

delectationem, quia habet in seipso delectationem perfectam in operatione virtutis; sed propter bonam operationem, ut scilicet eis benefaciat, et ut eos inspiciens benefacere delectetur, et ut etiam ab eis in benefaciendo adiuvetur. [...] Sed si loquamur de perfecta beatitudine quae erit in patria, non requiritur societas amicorum de necessitate ad beatitudinem [...] Sed ad bene esse beatitudinis facit societas amicorum." Thomas Aquinas, ST, I-II, 4, 8, ad corp.

342 "Ob motive oecumenica clare exprimitur quod cultus erga coelites essentialiter differt a cultu latreutico, soli Deo oblato." *Synposis*, 489.

343 "Nobilissima vero ratione unio nostra cum Ecclesia coelesti actuatur, cum, praesertim in sacra Liturgia [...] divinae maiestatis laudem socia exsultatione concelebramus [...] Eucharisticum ergo sacrificium celebrantes cultui Ecclesiae coelestis vel maxime iungimur [...]." LG, n. 50.

344 Cf. LG, n. 51.

345 "Ac tandem in capite VIII [...] specialis consideratio tribuitur B. Mariae Virgini, tum in mysterio Christi, cuius ipsa est mater, tum in mysterio Ecclesiae, cuius ipsa est maternalis et virginalis typus. In quo finali capite, coronidis instar, tota expositio de mysterio Ecclesiae velut recapitulatur." *Synopsis*, 484.

346 "In mysterio enim Ecclesiae, quae et ipsa iure mater vocatur et virgo, Beata Virgo Maria praecessit, eminenter et singulariter tum virginis tum matris exemplar praebens." LG, n. 63.

347 "Evidens est autem singularis dignitas Deiparae ex contactu suo cum ipsis Personis divinis." *Synopsis*, 490.

348 "Est simul mater, scilicet Christi ipsius secundum carnem, at etiam mater fratrum Eius cooperatione sua spirituali." *Synopsis*, 492.

349 "Quapropter etiam ut supereminens prorsusque singulare membrum Ecclesiae necnon eius in fide et caritate typus et exemplar [...]." LG, n. 53.

350 "[...] hoc summo munere ac dignitate ditatur ut sit Genetrix Dei Filii, ideoque praedilecta filia Patris necnon sacrarium Spiritus Sancti [...]," *Ibid.*

351 " [...] ne discrepantia appareat inter mulierem, matrem Christi in Evangeliis, et figuram B. Virginis qualiter in tractatione theologica exhibetur vel a populo christiano colitur." *Synposis*, 491.

352 CCC, n. 499.

353 "[...] scilicet fide et oboedientia, fidelitate et caritate." *Synopsis*, 492.

354 CCC, n. 972.

355 John Damascene, *Second Homily on the Dormition of Mary.*

[356] "Qui cultus, [...] singularis omnino quamquam est, essentialiter differt a cultu adorationis, qui Verbo incarnato aeque ac Patri et Spiritui Sancto exhibetur, eidemque potissimum favet." *LG*, n. 66.

[357] "[...] veram devotionem neque in sterili et transitorio affectu, neque in vana quadam credulitate consistere, sed a vera fide procedere [...] eiusque virtutum imitationem excitamur." *LG*, n. 67.

[358] "[...] secundum amicitiae proportionem, ut Deus impleat hominis voluntatem in salvatione alterius: licet quandoque possit habere impedimentum ex parte illius cuius aliquis sanctus iustificationem desiderat." Thomas Aquinas, ST, I-II, 114, 6, ad corp.

[359] "[...] vita, dulcedo, et spes nostra [...]," *Salve Regina*.

About the Author

Fr. Brian Thomas Becket Mullady is the son of an Air Force officer and was raised throughout the United States. He entered the Dominican Order in 1966 and was ordained in Oakland, California, in 1972. He has been a parish priest, high school teacher, retreat master, mission preacher, and university professor. He received his doctorate in sacred theology (STD) from the Angelicum University in Rome and was a professor there for six years. He has taught at several colleges and seminaries in the United States. He is currently a mission preacher and retreat master for the Western Dominican Province. He also teaches two months of the year at Holy Apostles Seminary in Cromwell, Connecticut. Fr. Mullady has had fourteen series on the EWTN Global Catholic Network. He is the author of four books and numerous articles and writes the answer column in *Homiletic and Pastoral Review*. He is also designated as an official Missionary of Mercy by Pope Francis.